D0232557

MKLM Library

The Art of Praying

The Principles and Methods
of Christian Prayer

Romano Guardini

The Art of Praying
The Principles and Methods of Christian Prayer

Formerly entitled
Prayer in Practice

SOPHIA INSTITUTE PRESS
Manchester, New Hampshire

The Art of Praying was originally published as *Vorschule des Betens* by Matthias-Grünewald Verlag, Mainz, Germany. Pantheon Books published this English translation by Prince Leopold of Loewenstein-Wertheim in 1957 as *Prayer in Practice*. This Sophia Institute Press edition is published by arrangement with Pantheon Books, a Division of Random House, Inc.

Copyright © 1957, 1985 Pantheon Books, A Division of Random House, Inc.

Printed in the United States of America

All rights reserved

Jacket design by Joan Barger

No part of this book may be reproduced, stored in a retrieval system, or transmitted in any form, or by any means, electronic, mechanical, photocopying, or otherwise, without the prior written permission of the publisher, except by a reviewer, who may quote brief passages in a review.

Sophia Institute Press

Box 5284, Manchester, NH 03108

1-800-888-9344

Nihil obstat: Joannes M. T. Barton, S.T.D., L.S.S., *Censor Deputatus*
Imprimatur: E. Morrogh Bernard, *Vicar General, Westmonasterii*
February 20, 1957

Library of Congress Cataloging-in-Publication Data

Guardini, Romano, 1885-1968
  [Vorschule des Betens. English]
  The art of praying : the principles and methods of Christian prayer :
formerly entitled Prayer in practice / Romano Guardini.
      p. cm.
  English translation originally published: New York, N.Y. :
    Pantheon, c1957.
  Includes bibliographical references.
  ISBN 0-918477-21-2
  1. Prayer—Christianity.   I. Title.
BV210.G8213   1994
248.3'2—dc20   94-6426 CIP

94 95 96 97 98 99 10 9 8 7 6 5 4 3 2

Table of Contents

The Art of Praying

The Principles and Methods
of Christian Prayer

Editor's Note: The biblical references in the following pages are based on the Douay-Rheims edition of the Old and New Testaments. Where appropriate, quotations from the Psalms have been cross-referenced with the differing enumeration in the Revised Standard Version using the following symbol: (RSV=).

Preparation and Form

The life and practice of prayer

It is often asserted that true prayer cannot be willed or ordered, but must flow spontaneously, like water from the spring, from within. If this does not happen, if it does not well up from our innermost being, one had better not pray at all, for forced prayer is untrue and unnatural.

This sounds, at first, convincing; however, if one has gained a fuller understanding of man's nature and religious life, one cannot wholly dismiss the suspicion that those who propound such views have never seriously concerned themselves with prayer. Undoubtedly, there is prayer which comes unprompted from within. For instance, some unexpected glad tidings may move a man to give thanks and praise to God; or, when in great distress, he may turn to Him whose love he does not doubt and who has the power to comfort and to help. There are times also when man experiences God's presence so vividly that he speaks to Him spontaneously. Or he suddenly becomes aware of the work of divine government behind some event and stands still, overawed.

The fact that these things do happen does not mean that they must inevitably happen. Life and destiny may stand like an impenetrable wall between man and God. The feeling of the holy presence may disappear so completely that man may think he has never experienced it. Happiness may cause him never to think of God, or affliction may shut off the inner vision. The dictum "sorrow teaches people to pray" is only half true, for it is equally true that adversity turns people away from prayer.

Prayer which springs from inner longing must, on the whole, be considered as the exception. Anyone proposing to build his religious life on this foundation would most probably give up prayer altogether. He would be like a person trying to base his life entirely on intuition and impressions, leaving aside order, discipline, and work. Such a life would be at the mercy of chance; it would become self-indulgent, arbitrary, fanciful; earnestness and steadfastness would vanish. The same would happen to prayer that relied exclusively on inner spontaneity. Anyone who takes his relationship to God seriously soon sees that prayer is not merely an expression of the inner life which will prevail on its own, but is also a service to be performed in faith and obedience. Thus it must be willed and practiced.

Establishing a regular schedule for prayer

It is of this practice of prayer that we shall speak here. Above all, it consists in saying one's prayers at certain fixed hours: in the morning before starting the tasks of the day and in the evening before retiring. In addition everyone should do what he thinks right, what he is able to do, and what suits his routine: perhaps grace before and after meals, the *Angelus*, a short collect before work, or a quiet moment in a church. An essential condition for this practice is to adopt the right attitude, both outwardly and inwardly: recollectedness at the beginning and discipline during prayer are essential, as is the right choice of words and texts, the learning of old, established forms of prayer such as contemplation, the Rosary, and others.

Self-deception about prayer

No hard-and-fast rules can be laid down for this; we shall discuss it more fully later. But whatever routine one may adopt, one should carry it out honestly and conscientiously. In matters of prayer we are only too apt to deceive ourselves because, generally speaking, man does not enjoy praying. He easily experiences boredom, embarrassment, unwillingness, or even hostility. Everything else appears to him more attractive and more important. He persuades himself that he has not got the time, that there are other more urgent things to do; but no sooner has he given up prayer than he applies himself to the most trivial tasks. We should stop lying to God. Better to say openly, "I do not wish to pray," than to make such excuses. Better not to resort to specious justifications such as, for instance, tiredness, but to declare, "I do not feel like praying." This may sound less decorous, but at least it is the truth which leaves the way open, whereas self-deception does not.

Prayer is essential to faith

But it is as well that we should remind ourselves that this is an important and serious matter. We should not be self-indulgent; we should do what duty and necessity require of us, and if it prove hard we should not hesitate to be a little stern with ourselves. Without prayer, faith becomes weak and the religious life atrophies. One cannot, in the long run, remain a Christian without praying, as one cannot live without breathing.

But is this really so? Is prayer really necessary? Or is it only for inactive, impractical, somewhat weak people who do not properly fit into life? Might one not even say on the basis of certain observations that there is something unnatural and musty about the world of praying people, something which repels the feeling of that which is vigorous and life-affirming? We shall examine later whether there is any truth in this assertion. Here we are merely discussing the fundamental question of whether prayer is a compelling necessity for the conduct of a true Christian life.

Prayer is essential to health

We may go further and ask whether it is not also a necessity from the point of view of ordinary health and well-being. There have been many noteworthy pronouncements to the effect that man runs a serious risk if his life is completely devoid of any activity which corresponds or is akin to prayer. Medical authorities point out that people whose attitude is exclusively extrovert, who are carried from one sensation to another, whose thoughts, conversation, work, struggles, and desires are mainly directed toward external goals, soon reach a state of exhaustion and confusion.

To prevent this, life must flow in two directions. It must renew itself from the inner roots, to gather there new strength and resilience. Modern man is in danger of losing his innermost center which gives stability to his personality and direction to his way of life. Behind the facade of talk and ceaseless activities he becomes unsure of himself; beneath his self-assured *persona* there is an ever increasing anxiety. To counteract this trend he must rediscover the point of inner support from which he can issue forth into the world and to which he may return again and again.

To regain inner stability it is not sufficient to spend weekends and holidays in the country. A holiday by the sea or in the mountains, no doubt, affords a measure of physical and mental recreation, but it is not true compensation and its effects are soon spent. What is required is a real counterbalance which is always effective. This cannot be found in purely intellectual pursuits. Poetry, music, and the arts are in themselves not sufficient; nor is philosophy or any other mental activity. Doctors know this, but to the question of what should be done they usually have no precise answer. Some of them, however, will advocate something in the nature of spiritual or religious practice, some form of contemplative exercise: in short, some form of prayer. This, however, is difficult where faith lacks conviction, for prayer helps only if it is practiced not merely for the sake of its possible effects, but for the sake of the inner relationship to God. It is important that those who believe in this relationship, or who are aware of it, should constantly renew it.

As to the reproach of weakness and ineffectualness — which is frequently leveled against those who seek support in prayer — it must be said that true prayer demands humility. This is not weakness but truth. Strength without reverence for the majesty of the Holy — strength without humility — is utterly barren.

Faith is a prerequisite for prayer

Man needs prayer to remain spiritually healthy. But prayer can spring only from living faith. On the other hand — and this completes the circle — faith can remain alive only when nourished by prayer. Prayer, therefore, is not merely an activity which one may practice or leave without faith being affected. On the contrary, prayer is the most fundamental expression of faith — that is, communion with God, on whom our faith is centered.

There may be times when prayer falters, but, in the long run, faith without prayer is impossible — as life is impossible without breath.

Does not this analogy of breath contradict the argument? Life could not exist without breath, and therefore while there is life, breath continues unceasingly; no conscious willing, no practice are required to maintain it. But this is only half true, for we know that there is neglected, atrophied, and diseased breathing, and that it may have to be invigorated and cured by exercises. Let us leave it at that for the moment, and agree that breath is an involuntary action as is the beating of the heart.

The analogy of breath and prayer, however, becomes exact if we consider what kind of life the breath of which we speak sustains, and how this life is constituted. Faith teaches that into our first "old" life God planted a seed which is meant to unfold — *the seed of a new life*. This seed is weak, vulnerable, uncertain, as all living things are in the beginning. The old life lies heavily on it, holding it down, inhibiting its unfolding.

The life with which our feelings and thoughts are directly concerned — the life of natural man with his physical and mental necessities — asserts itself openly. The other life, however, is hidden; it rarely penetrates the threshold of cognition; it must be believed in and nurtured.

Hence the danger that we may neglect it and allow it to be smothered. While the natural breath continues vigorously, the hidden one emanating from the Holy Spirit may become weaker and may even come to a halt. This new inner life is given to us by God to tend as the life of the newborn child is given to the mother. We must therefore ask ourselves what value we place on this life and act accordingly. We must do what is necessary to maintain and develop it, carrying out the task which Truth demands of us — the Truth of the Word is God, which illumines and purifies human knowledge.

The need to prepare for prayer

Man's attitude toward religious matters is full of disturbing contradictions. Man needs God and he knows it; he seeks Him, his Creator by whose power he lives. On the other hand, man does not like to acknowledge this link: he evades and resists God. This contradiction also shows itself in man's attitude to prayer. As soon as he acknowledges the holy duty of prayer and submits to it, he experiences the truth and finds consolation and happiness. Yet he evades prayer as much as possible.

There are many reasons for this — the main one being that we cannot perceive God, or to put it more exactly, we cannot perceive Him in the manner in which we perceive objects and people. The latter are there before us; they act and they affect us; our senses take them in; instinct and will react, and thus our relations with them develop almost automatically. God is before us, more real than anything else, and yet He is hidden. He is seen by the inner eye of faith; He is known by the heart which loves Him. But the inner vision is often clouded and the heart is dull; thus we have no immediate experience of God. Communion with Him through mere faith, reaching as it were through the emptiness and darkness of the unknown, is extremely difficult.

Natural inclinations must not govern prayer life

It is a great mystery that man, whose life springs from God, should have such difficulty in communing with Him; that indeed he should experience disinclination to do so and should seize on any pretext to evade Him. If man merely followed his natural feelings he would soon have no desire to pray. It would, however, be highly dangerous to conclude that this is his proper condition and that he had better accept it, rather than try to change it. This could be right for him only if his natural feelings were truly reliable, especially in religious matters. But this is not so. Are a sick man's feelings a reliable standard of truth? Common sense tells us that his feelings may well be unreliable and that he should therefore, guided by superior knowledge — for instance, the judgment of an experienced doctor — establish a regime and persevere in it. In this manner and with time, his feelings may be restored to health. Only then will they be reliable. We are like the sick man; we are sick in our relationship to God and to the world. We cannot therefore make our natural feelings the true standard for our religious attitude, but must follow enlightened opinion in order to put ourselves and our feelings right. The supposed truthfulness which consists in doing what inclination demands is frequently an evasion of truth. In the practice of prayer, therefore, we must also endeavor to seek what is right and to do it loyally and, if need be, against our inclinations.

Prayer is only as good as the preparation for it

Above all, we must prepare ourselves for prayer. The same applies also to all worldly matters. No one with a serious task before him will approach it unprepared, but will concentrate on the demands he has to face. If we appreciate good music we shall not arrive at the performance at the last minute, allowing for no transition between the noise and unrest of the street and the opening bars of the concert. We shall be there in good time and hold ourselves ready for the beautiful experience before us. Anyone who has the right feeling for things which are great and important will, before tackling them, banish distraction and recollect himself inwardly.

The same must hold good for prayer — all the more since God, as we have said, is hidden and must be found in faith. Praying is an act of religious worship. The faculty which it must awaken and turn toward the object of worship — if this term may be used — is not merely that of thought and action, but the inmost *inwardness* of the soul: in other words, the very thing which in man corresponds to the mysterious holiness of God. In everyday life this inner faculty is silent or at best just faintly noticeable, for man is wholly occupied with the worldly aspects of his being, living as it were by his worldly powers. But if prayer is to be true, then that which belongs to the sphere of the holy must come into its own.

Therefore preparation is necessary and it is generally true to say that the prayer will be as good as the preparation for it. What this preparation aims at and how it should be undertaken can be examined under various headings, but above all under the heading of *recollectedness*.

Recollectedness as "composure and concentration"

Recollectedness, for one thing, means that man becomes *composed and concentrated*. Usually he is distracted by the diversity of objects and events, agitated by friendly or hostile contacts, assailed by desires, fear, care, or passion. He is constantly bent on achieving something, or on warding off something, on acquiring or rejecting, on building up or destroying. Man always wants something; and to want means to be on the way, either toward a goal or away from a danger. This has been so ever since man existed and is even more so with modern man. Man likes to think of himself as active, striving, and creative. In this he is only partly right. He would in fact be even more right if he thought of himself as a restless being, incapable of standing still or of concentrating; as one who uses up people, things, thoughts, and words without, however, finding fulfillment; as a being who has lost the link with the center and who, with all his knowledge and abilities, is a victim of chance.

This restless being wants to pray. Can he do it? Only if he steps out of the stream of restlessness and composes himself.

This means discarding roaming desires and concentrating on that thing alone which, for the time being, is the only one that matters. He must detach himself and say, "Now there is nothing which concerns me, except prayer. The next ten minutes" (or whatever time he may have allocated to it) "are reserved for this. Everything else is excluded; I am completely free and dedicated to this one task," and he must be completely honest in this, for man is an artful creature and the artfulness of his heart asserts itself in religious matters.

No sooner has he started to pray than, conjured up by his inner unrest, all sorts of other things clamor for attention: a task at work, a conversation, an errand, a newspaper, a book. All these suddenly appear most important, and prayer seems a sheer waste of time. But no sooner has he stopped praying than there is plenty of time, and he fritters it away with useless activities. To recollect oneself means to overcome this deception which springs from unrest and to become still; to free oneself of everything which is irrelevant, and to hold oneself at the disposal of God, who alone matters now.

Recollectedness as "becoming present"

We may express this differently by saying that what matters is that man should *become present*. This unrest which grips us when we are about to pray may also be defined as an urge to be somewhere else. We can yield to this urge by getting up and going, either into the next room or into the street or to the office; or we may look out of the window or take up a book or think of something else: of people or professional matters, or of anything that comes into our mind. Always this inner unrest drives us away from the place where we should be, namely, the *here* and the *duty*.

This is the place where things really matter, where one must hold one's ground; the place where the living God calls to the self — the place of obedience.

In this exacting stillness man begins to feel uncomfortable and tries to run away. Always he flees from the holy *here* where the call reaches him and where everything is in its right place. It would appear that the more firmly man is rooted in the world, the more adrift he becomes from the place which really matters.

If he wants to pray, he must recall himself from everything and everywhere and become and remain present. This *remaining* is difficult, for only on rare occasions do we meet with an experience so definite and compelling as to hold us and make us willing to remain for awhile. Yet everything depends on this ability to stand still and to be present with full inner awareness.

Recollectedness as "unified"

The basic meaning of the word *recollected* is "to be unified, gathered together." A glance at our life will show how much we lack this aptitude. We should have a fixed center which, like the hub of a wheel, governs our movements and from which all our actions go out and to which they return; a standard, also, or a code by which we distinguish the important from the unimportant, the end from the means, and which puts actions and experiences into their proper order; something stable, unaffected by change and yet capable of development, which makes it clear to us who we are and how matters stand with us. We lack this; we, the men of today, lack it more than did those who lived in earlier ages.

This becomes evident in our attempts to pray. Spiritual teachers speak of *distraction* as that state in which man lacks poise and unity, that state in which thoughts flit from object to object, in which feelings are vague and unfocused and the will ineffective.

Man in this state is not really a person who speaks or who can be spoken to, but merely an uncoordinated bundle of thoughts, feelings, and sensations. Recollectedness means that he who prays gathers himself together, directs his attention to what he is doing, draws in all thought — a painstaking task — so as to dedicate himself to prayer as a unified whole. This is the state in which he may, when the call comes to him, answer in the words of Moses, "Here I am."[1]

Recollectedness as "awakenedness"

And a fourth and last meaning: *to recollect oneself* is to awaken. With people who are not recollected there is always something tense, some preoccupation; and as soon as this preoccupation and tension lessens, they become all of a sudden empty and listless. When there is no object which draws them, no motive which pushes or stimulus which agitates them, then their activity flags and a strange desolation takes its place. Outward restlessness often goes together with inner listlessness. Indeed, the latter determines the peculiar character of the former. A recollected person, however, who is able to concentrate, to become still, and to withdraw into himself, is inwardly *awake*. The states of quietness and inner alertness belong together, supporting and determining each other.

Therefore anyone able to recollect himself, to be still and present, overcomes the inner brooding and heaviness. He lifts himself up and makes himself light, free, and clear. He awakens the inner attention so that it may focus itself on its object. He clears the inner eye so that it may see true. He calls upon the inner preparedness so that contact becomes possible.

[1] Exod. 3:4.

Recollectedness is not an isolated condition but the mind's right and proper state, the state which enables man to establish the right relationship to men and things. The nature of recollectedness varies in accordance with the ends to which it is directed, and what has been said about it so far does not exhaust this subject.

It is not easy to establish this state of mind, especially if, after initial attempts, interest flags and inner confusion rises to the surface. We say it is not easy; ought we not rather ask whether it is at all possible? Are we not so inextricably entangled in the web of external and internal causation that we can only resign ourselves to being as we are and must leave it to chance whether we achieve a greater degree of inner unity? Does not the attempt to achieve this unity resemble the vain efforts of a man who tries to pull himself out of a swamp by his own forelock? Does not such an attempt presuppose that we are, simultaneously, within ourselves and outside ourselves, and thus able to get a hold on ourselves?

This sounds like a strange question but it is justified. The answer to it is "Yes, we are also outside." It is of the very nature of man as a *person* that he is, at one and the same time, within and without; that he grows out of himself and yet has control over himself; that he *is* and yet can renew himself out of himself.

The way in which this happens cannot be discussed here, as it would necessitate entering fully into the whole vast subject of the nature of man. We therefore ask you to believe that it is so, and if you have the courage to act on this, you will find that it is true. The mysterious place into which you must step if you want to get hold of yourself does exist. Take the step and you will know it.

It is not merely a place; it is a center of power; it is something quite distinct from that realm of your being which is constantly changing, fleeting, and dissolving. It is substantial and everlasting. It is you: your *self*, your proper being. From there and through it you can still your unrest. There you can take root and be present;

15

from there you can gather in all that is dispersed; you can lift the weight off your mind and lighten your darkness.

Recollectedness is the beginning of prayer

Prayer must begin with recollectedness, but it is not easy. How little of it we normally possess becomes painfully clear as soon as we make the first attempt. When we try to compose ourselves, unrest doubles in intensity, not unlike the manner in which at night, when we try to sleep, cares or desires assail us with a force they lack during the day. When we want to be truly *present* we feel how powerful are the voices trying to call us away. As soon as we try to be unified and to obtain mastery over ourselves, we experience the full impact and meaning of distraction. And when we try to be awake and receptive to the holy object, we are seized by an inertness which lowers our spirit. All this is inevitable; we must endure it and persevere; otherwise we shall never learn to pray.

Everything depends on this state of recollectedness. No effort to obtain it is ever wasted. And even if the whole duration of our prayer should be applied to this end only, the time thus used would have been well employed. For recollectedness itself is prayer. In times of distress, illness, or great exhaustion, it can be most beneficial to content oneself with such a *prayer of recollectedness*. It will calm, fortify, and help. Finally, if at first we achieve no more than the understanding of how much we lack in inner unity, something will have been gained, for in some way we would have made contact with that center which knows no distraction.

The spiritual realm of prayer

Recollectedness opens the door to prayer, reveals its inner "space." The term is not used here in the literal sense, for this space has no extension; it is neither within nor without. It is a realm of the spirit. But again it is not that realm of the spirit where the images of thought and the intentions of the will dwell, but the realm of the Holy Spirit. It comes into existence only in communion with God. We might liken it to the common ground on which people find themselves who have established a close mutual relationship. It emerges and it disappears in accordance with the esteem, reverence, or love which the two people feel for each other and is as wide or deep as are their feelings. That God has revealed Himself to us, dwells among us, gives us His love, and that we are able to stand before Him in our faith — this constitutes the holy place or ground.

God summons us to recollectedness

One might perhaps say that recollectedness itself in due course brings about the spiritual condition, the holy ground which, in turn, enables man to say, "God is here." This is the sequence of events as it appears to our limited perception. But in fact, the attainment of recollectedness, the creation of the necessary spiritual condition, the presence of God and man's communion with Him, form one simultaneous whole. Indeed, man can recollect himself only because God turns to him. The very words "Here I am" could not be uttered by him if God were not present to summon him and indicate the holy ground to him.

God enables us to discover our own deepest selves

It is God who by His presence creates the holy ground which man discovers by recollecting himself and where, having done so, he stands. God shows man the place where he really belongs, where he will find himself and his true world; where the call can reach him and where he must answer it. Recollectedness, there-fore, is the condition which enables man to say, "God is here, the Living, the Holy, of whom Revelation speaks, and here also am I." But not the vague *I* of everyday life, that confused something which sits down at table, walks through the streets of the town, works at the office, but the real *I* — the *self*. This is the *I* which makes me responsible for my existence, that *I* — humble and poor though he may be — which is unique and irreplaceable and which God had in mind when He created me and to which the words "God and my soul and nothing else in the world" apply. That *I* awakens only before God.

In the presence of God awakens that with which He has endowed man so that man may respond to Him: *spiritual* con-sciousness. Man does not live by the use of his conscious faculties alone; his many and varied needs and aspirations can be satisfied only by drawing on sources lying much deeper in his being. The answer to a routine problem or anxiety over a professional diffi-culty, the feeling engendered by a great work of art or the devotion to a beloved person — all these reactions rise from equally varied depths which lie close to our essential being.

These sources, however, cannot be tapped at will. Each one will respond only to the need or the object appropriate to it. Many of us do not know what dwells in us and of what we are capable until the right call reaches us. This same condition may be said to apply to spiritual consciousness, which answers to the call of the mystery behind the appearance of things and to the hidden mean-ing of events; to that which, although in the world, is not of the world — namely, the continuous self-revelation of God. Awak-ened by His touch, guided by His call, spiritual consciousness seeks Him: this is religion. But it remains unsure, confused, full of errors until God speaks explicitly, first through His messengers and then through His Son, Jesus Christ. If man puts his trust in this message he reaches God. This happens in rightly informed prayer. This is the holy encounter. In it awakens not only the religious consciousness but a new and higher consciousness, which we might call the spiritual heart of the child of God.

God reveals Himself to us in prayer

On this holy ground the reality of God becomes manifest. It may happen that man experiences it suddenly and is overcome by its grandeur and flooded by its proximity. If this happens, he knows that he is receiving the great and intimate mystery of prayer. He must receive it with reverence and guard it well. But such an event is rare indeed and more often than not nothing happens. The God of whom the worshipper had said "He is here" remains silent and hidden. Then the prayer, supported by faith alone, must go out into this silent darkness and maintain itself there.

God's being differs from our being

In recollectedness the worshipper says, "God is here and here also am I." In saying this, he becomes aware of an important distinction. He realizes that in the two sentences "God is here" and "Here am I" the verb *to be* has different meanings. Differences of meaning also attach to it in ordinary life. If someone asks, "What is in this room?" and I answer, "In the center stands a table, on the windowsill is a rose, on the carpet lies a dog, before me sits my friend," then I have said of all these various things and living beings that they *are* in the room. But they are not there in the same manner. The plant which lives and grows *is* more than and *is* different from the table; the dog who knows me and answers my call also *is*, but he is more so than the plant, and in a different way. But man also *is* — differently and more intensely, being endowed with freedom and dignity and able to reason and to love. And different men possess, to varying degrees, the power and the manner of *being*.

Someone enters the room and is there, but he is there only in the sense that one has to take notice of his physical presence and position in space. Another one, however, is there to a degree which demands that we pay attention to what he says. A third will, by his mere presence, become the center of interest. From this, what has been said about the different meanings of the verb *to be* becomes clear. God *is*, as nobody and nothing is. He is from Himself and by reason of Himself. Thus He alone has substance; He alone verily *is*. The Scriptures express that He is *the Lord*. He does not become the Lord by virtue of His power over things; He is Lord of His very nature — the absolute Being.

I, however, am not from myself and by reason of myself. I am through Him: not being, but existing by His grace; not absolute, but contingent. Between my way of being and His, the coordinating conjunction *and* has no place. The sentence "God and I are" is devoid of meaning. Were I to maintain it in all seriousness, I would be blaspheming.

My being stands in an entirely different relationship to God than does the being of a creature to that of his fellow. I am only *before* Him and *through* Him.[2] In a state of true recollectedness, one experiences this truth. One will have learnt something very important when one knows that one *is* before God, and in reality *only* before Him. It is something very great; it can become frightening and at the same time joyous, and we shall see that on this realization rests one of the fundamental acts of prayer, that is, adoration.

[2] Cf. Rom. 11:36; Eph. 4:6.

Prayer brings us to know the face of God

Who, then, is this God, toward whom man may, in a proper state of recollectedness, direct his thoughts — direct them because He Himself enables man to do so? He is not only the all-embracing *ineffable*, the *mystery* of existence, the *ground of the world*, or whatever term one may use to designate that which cannot be named. All these are attributes of God, but it is merely the breath of God, the vibration with which He penetrates the universe. God Himself is more: not merely meaning or idea, but reality; not only the depth, structure, center, width of the universe, but Being pure and absolute; not mere potentiality, but *Himself*. The beginning and end of all Revelation is contained in that made to Moses on Mount Horeb when God revealed Himself and Moses said: "I shall go to the children of Israel, and say to them: 'The God of your fathers hath sent me to you.' If they should say to me: 'What is His name?' what shall I say to them?" God said to Moses: "*I Am Who Am.*" He said: "Thus shalt thou say to the children of Israel: '*He Who Is* hath sent me to you.' "[3] In this solemn moment God dispenses with all such attributes as *the mighty, the just, the merciful* and calls Himself as He is, in Himself responsible to Himself alone, free — the God who *is*. It is this being in His own right that is His essence.

God is Himself *Person* — not only the most powerful, exalted, purest person, but the *Person in itself*. When we spoke of the reality of God we said that it was of a kind which precluded finite reality from being mentioned in the same context. *God is*, but man is only through Him and before Him. Here we say that God is the *essential person*, but man becomes person only when God calls him.

[3] Exod. 3:13-14.

When we refer to another person we use the personal pronoun *he* or *she*. But when we spontaneously say *He* without any personal reference, we can mean only God; and if from the very depth of our being we call "Thou" we are, in fact, calling Him. For whether we know it or not, God is closer and dearer to us than any other being.

To Him we pray. The relationship with God into which man enters in prayer is frequently referred to in the Scriptures. The beautiful expression "the face of God" is used in this connection.

This must be understood metaphorically. God has no face as we understand it, for He has no body as we understand it. But man is made in the image of God — the whole man, not only his soul. Everything, therefore, every feature and attribute which is part of the wholeness of man is a manifestation of God. Hence, in a manner beyond all human conception, there is something in God which corresponds to what in man we call *face*.

The face of man reflects his inner self; it expresses his personality and his ability to "face" others in friendship or hostility, in love or hatred. (We say that "Man faces his destiny" or that he "visualizes danger" or that "he looks favorably on someone." All these phrases metaphorically describe attitudes which man can adopt because he is a *person*, a being endowed with free will and responsibility.) Man's face also expresses his faculty of opening himself to others and of establishing *rapport* with others. All these faculties — in a manner which surpasses human understanding — are present in God, and that is why the Scriptures say that "God lets his face shine upon man"[4] or that He "sets his face against"[5] those who disobey Him.

[4] Pss. 30:17; 66:2; 79:20 (RSV: Pss. 31:16; 67:1; 80:19).
[5] Lev. 17:10; 20:3, 5.

In Psalm 26, the mystery of the divine countenance is expressed forcefully and with great poetic beauty: "My heart hath said to Thee: my face hath sought Thee. Thy face, O Lord, will I still seek. Turn not away Thy face from me; decline not in Thy wrath from Thy servant. Be Thou my helper; forsake me not. Do not Thou despise me, O God my savior. For my father and my mother have left me: but the Lord hath taken me up."[6]

We should seek the face of God

The first step into prayer is self-recollection. The second is visualizing (before the inner eye) God's reality. The third is seeking His holy face. In this the worshipper tries to establish, or rather to give expression and effect to, the *I-thou* relationship with God which is man's birthright. God (to whom I speak in prayer) knows me not merely as one among countless others but as *myself* in the uniqueness and irreplaceableness of my person. Although I may be as nothing in His sight, yet it has pleased Him to call me and to establish a relationship in which I am alone with Him. Into this mystery of love one enters through prayer.

This is the meaning of the injunction that man should seek the "face of God,"[7] or, as one may also put it — and this is a new mystery — "the heart of God." It is not easy. When I begin to pray there is around me the distraction of the world and within me the turmoil of my thoughts and feelings. Apart from that, there is nothing but emptiness. Although faith tells me that God is present, I am rarely conscious of this. Although He is everywhere, He is — if one may put it thus — always just out of reach, hidden from me. In this concealment, darkness, and void, my faith must seek

---

[6] Ps. 26:8-10 (RSV: Ps. 27:8-10).

[7] Ps. 104:4 (RSV: Ps.105:4).

out His countenance and His heart so that I may direct my prayer to Him. I must establish the inner point of contact and hold on to it, when — as constantly happens — it tries to elude me. Again and again, prayer tends to dwindle into mere monologue or a vague recitation of words. It is an essential part of the preparation to guard against this, and it demands as well constant vigilance during the prayer itself. Prayer should be an address to God and a dialogue.

Before God's face man receives his own true countenance. The visible features which make up the face of man are but the outward layer of the real face. Beneath these features are the inner form, the character, the informing spirit, and the indwelling soul. Often enough the face of man is but a mask. How this mask can spring into life we have occasion to observe when a man's face lights up in a conversation which interests him or in an encounter which moves him. It is as though his face, his real face, suddenly disclosed itself from within. These are natural things but they point to divine things. The face which matters before the sight of God, man does not possess in his own right; it is given to him by God. Only in speaking to Him do I become that *self* which He meant me to grow into when He created and redeemed me. Only in prayer does my real face unfold and assume its own true features.

The time of prayer

We have spoken of the practice of prayer. It includes what can be termed the *inner* discipline, the mental attitude which must be established and maintained as an essential precondition for this practice. Now we must speak of discipline in the more usual meaning of the term, that is, outward procedure and method. Above all, there is the natural rhythm of time. It is based on the rhythm of light which also governs the activities of man and the events of life: day and night, the working week and Sunday, the year with its seasons. This rhythm must find expression also in prayer.

With the morning the day renews itself; with the evening it comes to a close. In the former the beginning of life — birth — is symbolized. The latter symbolizes and presages the end — death. In between lie work and struggle, endeavor and fate, growth, fertility, and perils. All this finds expression in morning prayers and evening prayers. Without these prayers the day would lack proper form.

From the phases of the moon, the month and the week emerge. Six days of the week are dedicated to work, one to rest. On working days man is bound by duty; on the seventh day he is free. This is the law of the week instituted by Him who made man and the universe. Together with this natural law of the seventh day He has ordained the spiritual law of the Lord's day. It is revealed that God achieved the work of the creation in six days and rested on the seventh. Behind this seventh day, therefore, there is the mystery of God's rest.

God's rest, not man's rest, is the meaning of Sunday, and from the former the latter derives its justification. Man must open himself to this significance. To the mystery of God's rest another mystery is added: that of the Resurrection of Christ. It crowns the meaning of the Lord's day with the victory of redemption and the victory over death. The light of the Resurrection fills Easter Sunday and from there is shed onto every Sunday of the year.

Sunday, therefore, is the day of God and, for this very reason, the day of man. Its meaning has been largely forgotten. In our modern age it has become a day of vaguely festive character and ultimately merely an occasion for recreation and pleasure.

It is not easy to say how this day may be restored to its proper status in an age which has lost the feeling of its true significance.

Here is a task which concerns everyone: to reinstate Sunday earnestly, yet without narrow-mindedness or compulsion, as a day of homage to the Creator and Redeemer of the World and at the same time as a day of rejoicing before the eyes of God. This is a task which must be tackled, not from without, but from within: by allowing the mind to dwell upon the mystery of this day and trying to comprehend how intimate are its links with our natural and spiritual life, by opening ourselves to its beauty and asking what can be done to give it its proper place in our own personal lives and in the life of the family. Then in accordance with the degree of our understanding, the appropriate effort must be made.

It should be emphasized here how important for Sunday is the Saturday evening before. According to the view of the Church, every day begins on the preceding evening, and this is justified. The day begins with the awakening; the quality of awakening will depend on the quality of sleep which preceded it. The sleep, however, is determined by what immediately precedes it. If, therefore, we want to approach Sunday in the right frame of mind, we must begin to prepare ourselves on Saturday evening.

The overall pattern of transition in time is set by the year and its seasons; it comprises month, week, and day and is determined by the phases of sunlight, the awakening, the flowering, the ripening, and the decline of life.

Its religious expression is the liturgical year of the Church, in which the events in the life of Christ are linked to the course of the solar year. Thus the memory of the life of Christ is constantly renewed and the redemption re-experienced.

Yearly, during Advent and Christmastide, the mind is stirred afresh by the memory of our Lord's appearance on earth; and then again during Lent and Easter by the memory of his Passion and Resurrection; again at Pentecost, which commemorates the descent of the Holy Spirit. Finally, during the many weeks after

Pentecost we follow the events of the ministry of Christ and share in the expectation of His second coming, right up to the last Sunday of the Church year which presages the Last Judgment. All this should find expression in our own personal religious life.

Aids to prayer

In former days people regularly read the family Bible. Through its pages the great events and figures of the redemption entered into their personal lives. Nowadays that intimate relationship has largely disappeared and it is important that we should try to re-establish it. By the study of the liturgy, the reading of appropriate books, and by establishing suitable forms of worship at home, we can do much to give new meaning and content to our prayers.

The place for prayer

In earlier days, the very layout of the living space of the community was an important factor in creating a well-ordered religious life. Indeed it may be said that the faith dictated the spatial order of the life of the community. If we consider the parish as the smallest unit of the social organization, it was the church which formed its center. Around it were the houses, each serving both as home and place of work for the family. Beyond were the fields and woods providing the common space of creative life. Running through all these sections and, as it were, knitting them together were chapels, shrines, the cemetery, and wayside crosses.

The house itself was blessed and adorned with Christian symbols. There was the crucifix, in front of which prayers were said.

This order has largely disappeared. There is no more a common Christian ground or space providing the natural background of religious life. It is therefore up to every Christian to create the right background for himself and his family. But since conditions in which people live differ so greatly, it is impossible to lay down general rules.

Above all, the church itself should assume new meaning and importance, not only as the place of communal worship, but as the house of the Father in which we are at home. We should cultivate this concept of the church as a home which we may visit on our daily rounds in order to find peace, recollectedness, comfort, courage, and recreation. In the home itself the idea of the consecrated place should be revived. But this is more difficult, especially when there is shortage of space, or where other members of the family show indifference or reluctance. All the same it should be possible to establish some kind of a sanctuary, be it only the corner of a room in which hangs a crucifix, in front of which one may sit down, or a holy picture on the wall which one approaches with special reverence.

A holy picture is more than a mere memento. Obviously it is not Christ Himself or the Mother of the Lord or the saint whom it depicts; we must beware of such fantasies. At the same time it is *more* than a mere symbol or reminder; and this *more* can become a force and influence in the life of the family, a force which reminds, warns, and orders. The family prayers should be said in front of the crucifix or picture; it should be adorned with flowers and generally held in reverence.

We should, however, guard against anything which is too fanciful or anything which imposes on others. We should do what we consider right and dignified without attracting too much attention and embarrassing others.

The world belongs to God and to Him also belongs its small counterpart, the home. It is, therefore, "meet and just" that His dominion should be given visible expression there. But ultimately the real Christian place is not a fixed location in space but something constantly emerging anew out of God's relationship to man. It is the sanctuary of our innermost heart where God is always present if we will but answer His call. Wherever else we are, we can be there too. However lacking we are in external space, this is a place to which we can always repair.

Prayers in our ordinary routine

The normal routine and events of everyday life themselves provide proper opportunities for religious observance. In former ages these daily events were imbued with religious significance which found appropriate expression. Little of this still remains, especially in big cities. It must therefore be left to the individual to re-establish these religious customs and, perhaps, to introduce new ones.

Among the few that have remained is the saying of grace before and after meals. Whenever it is possible to follow this custom without causing embarrassment, it should be done — standing, with reverence, and with the use of a suitable text.

In the dawn of civilization the meal had religious significance. It symbolized the communion with the Deity, and through it, the communion among the participants. There may be occasions when we discover some remnants of this symbolic meaning, expressed by a peculiarly reverent frame of mind (for which there is no obvious external cause) at the beginning of a meal.

Most people will agree that there is a world of difference between merely sitting down at table with others in order to enjoy good food, and reverently receiving food from the hands of God and giving thanks for it. Grace before and after meals in no way detracts from the pleasure and the naturalness of eating; on the contrary, it adds something to the meal — something which is fresh and holy.

For as long as possible mothers should say morning and evening prayers together with their children and should see to it that this moment of prayer is one of real reverence and self-recollection, despite the hustle and cares of the day. Into this prayer they should weave the events of family life with its joys, cares, and sorrows, thereby bringing before God the little community which, at that instant, speaks for the whole of mankind. The effect of a short act of worship such as this cannot be overestimated.

The whole of life is a challenge to prayer. Happy events call for one kind of prayer; sad events for another. Progress and success, care and distress, illness and recovery, birth and death: everything that happens in life must find expression in prayer and determine its nature. We must become more sensitive and perhaps — if we may put it thus — more inventive. Prayer should not always be restricted to the selfsame thoughts and words while life passes by in all its diversity.

We must bring everything that happens in our life before God as before a master or friend, or rather as before a father to whom everything matters which concerns us. We must show it to Him, thank Him, seek for strength and enlightenment, ask for His help, and seek repose with Him.

The duration of prayer

A few remarks should now be made about the duration of prayer. Above all, sufficient time must be allotted for it to start, to unfold, and to reach its termination. If prayer is too short, it assumes the character of something unimportant, and thereby becomes irreverent. Its component parts, thoughts and words, cannot fully come into their own; they quickly lose their virtue, and the spirit soon wearies of empty reciting. On the other hand, if something really urgent is likely to demand our attention, or if we are really too exhausted, we should not choose that particular moment for prayer. But let us remind ourselves of what has been said about the artfulness of the human heart, which is always on the lookout for plausible excuses. It happens over and over again that we catch ourselves frittering away the time which a moment before seemed too precious to be used on prayer.

The posture of prayer

One last point — the outward attitude. Here again much has been lost which is essential to the proper performance of prayer. In olden times people knew that outward bearing and behavior were not superficial things. They become superficial only when they have lost their inner meaning. Gesture reaches from the hand back to the heart. Outward bearing is rooted in inner attitude. It expresses what lives within, what the heart feels and the mind intends. Conversely it can itself affect the inner life, giving it stability and form.

It is therefore not a matter of indifference what outward attitude we adopt when praying. If there are compelling reasons, we may say our prayers in any posture; otherwise we should assume an attitude which gives outward expression to the reverence we owe to God, for it is not only the spirit which should pray, but man as a whole.

A proper outward manner, in its turn, fosters the right inner attitude and helps us to be reverent and recollected. The most correct way to pray is in the kneeling position. But we must kneel down properly, not — as so many of us do — in a half-sitting attitude. Kneeling is — and is meant to be — a posture of discipline, not of comfort, and anybody can maintain it for a little while. We ask much more of ourselves when it comes to sport or other physical exercise.

Another worthy attitude is standing upright. The early Chris-tians practiced it, but it has now largely been given up. We should adopt it again, for it expresses inner intent as well as dignity, and thus may help us to overcome depression and faintheartedness. Even as a mere expression of right intent — there are times when words of prayer do not come easily — this posture is beneficial; it expresses: "I am standing before Thee."

To be seated upright and still is an equally proper position for prayer. It is especially suited to contemplation or for moments of quiet devotion.

As important as these outward attitudes is what could be called the invisible attitude, which can be practiced in the street, at work, or even at social gatherings. This inner bearing by which the Christian, amidst the turmoil of the world, acknowledges the relationship between God and man, has great dignity and great beauty.

But there should be no ostentation or priggishness in this; and this proviso holds good as well for everything that has been said hitherto. It is deplorable if prayer loses its inner meaning or if its outward form lacks dignity; but it is equally deplorable to "show off" in prayer.

The gestures of prayer

When outward gesture expresses religious intent a holy symbol emerges. The sign of the Cross by which we open and close our prayer is such a symbol — a symbol, moreover, which has assumed a meaning in its own right.

What has been said about prayer in general also holds good for the sign of the Cross. It is the expression of the Christian faith and in itself an act of worship. At the same time it is something which exercises a powerful influence on man. By making the sign of the

Cross, we signify our acceptance of and adherence to the New Covenant, and our absolute faith in its holy power. It is important, therefore, that we should rightly understand and rightly make this holy sign.

2

The Reality of God
and the Basic Acts of Prayer

Recollectedness and the divine presence

On the holy ground to which we gain access in the state of recollectedness, the divine presence becomes manifest. To approach this divine reality is thus the prime task and toil of prayer; the second task is to hold firm in the holy presence and to comply with its exacting demands.

Toilsome prayer is yet worthy prayer

We have used the word *toil* deliberately because prayer can really be toil. At times, as we have said, prayer comes easily and as the heart's own language. But generally speaking and with the majority of people, this is not so. Mostly it must be willed and practiced, and the toil of this practice derives partly from the fact that we do not *experience* the real presence of God. Instead of experiencing His presence, the worshipper is conscious of a void;

35

in consequence everything else appears to him more urgent, more real. He must therefore persevere.

Anyone who says that prayer has nothing to offer him, that he feels no urge to pray, or that his prayer "does not ring true" and that therefore he had better leave it, misses the essential point of prayer. To be able to persevere through the hours of emptiness has a special value which cannot be replaced by the most inspired prayer at some other time. Only he who takes his faith seriously can continue to speak through the darkness without receiving any response — he *knows* that he is heard by Him to whom he speaks.

God may reveal Himself in the void

There are different kinds of voids. There is the void which is caused by the lack of something — the void of nonexistence. But there is another void, a void which is vibrant with being.

These two kinds are not always easily distinguishable. There are times when it seems that the void we experience when praying is the one of nonexistence. No wonder that we feel discouraged and find ourselves tempted to give up not only prayer, but belief in God altogether.

This is a testing of our faith, for as the song of praise in the *Sanctus* tells us: "Full are the heavens and the earth of the majesty of His glory." But we cannot see Him: although He is present, not merely as the stones and the trees are present, but present in a very special, intimate way, close to us, abiding with us — we cannot see Him. This very earth, which is full of the majesty of His glory, also acts as a veil to truth which our senses cannot penetrate.

Into this void of not-seeing, not-hearing, and not-experiencing, there may at times enter something, something inexpressible and yet significant — a hint of meaning amidst apparent nothingness, a meaning which prevails over the nothingness. It happens more frequently than one would expect and one should pay attention to it.

This breath, this vibration, is the manifestation of God, faint and intangible though it is, it can support our faith, so that we may persevere.

If faith perseveres the void may suddenly be filled, for God is not a mere fantasy, idea, or feeling, but the all-pervading reality. He does not dwell above us indifferent in the blissful remoteness of celestial spheres, but with us. To Him who is the all-free, the all-mighty, there are no barriers, not even the coldness of our hearts; and He will reveal Himself to those who persevere in faith.

If God were only an idea, even the supreme idea, we should be justified if we turned in preference to the diversity of *particulars*: to living people and to the earth in all its beauty and sorrow. But He is the living God who spoke thus: "Behold, I stand at the gate, and knock. If any man shall hear my voice, and open to me the door, I will come in to him."[8]

The reality of God can make itself felt as a mere breath or the mighty flood which completely fills man. It is experienced in our innermost soul, by the loftiest heights of our spirit, and by all that is most pure in our being. It is unique and simple and yet possesses the most diverse properties. That is why the masters of religious life speak of "spiritual organs of perception," that is, the inner eye and ear, the inner feeling and taste. They are referring to the different ways in which God can be experienced.

Yet prayer must persevere, independent of such experience. Should God reveal Himself, should it be vouchsafed to the worshipper to stand in the radiance of His light, he should be thankful and treasure the experience; but should all remain dark and void,

[8] Rev. 3:20.

he must hold on to faith alone and persevere. He may seek comfort in the prophecies at the end of the seven messages in the secret Revelation which speak of the victory in the darkness and misery of earthly life.[9]

God is the Holy One

Of all the attributes of God of which the Scriptures speak, the one that is paramount and which determines all others is holiness. What this holiness is, no one can know, not because it would be too hard for us to conceive or because it would, in its trail, bring a host of complex questions, but because it is a primary given fact — more precisely, *the* primary given fact. It is His basic nature, the first cause that determines His being. "To whom have ye likened me, or made me equal? saith the Holy One."[10]

In these words holiness proclaims itself as God's inmost essential being, thereby differentiating Him from all creation. Thus one cannot express what it is. One can but indicate: see, hark, and feel.

It is impossible to express in conceptual language what light is. But one can say what it does, what laws determine it, how it affects things, and what would happen if there were no light. But one cannot say what it is in itself. One can only say, "open your eyes and see."

God's holiness is that primary essential self wherein He has His being, and by which He is known. Every human being has diverse traits of character which can be described and named; but he has something more than those traits — not necessarily the sum of them, but something which flashes into the minds of those who love him, something ultimate and substantial which they regard as

[9] Rev. 2:3.
[10] Isa. 40:25.

being *him*, as constituting his true being. In the same manner we must regard God's holiness as His inmost essential being.

People, things, and events are earthly and of this world. God is unearthly; He is transcendent and mysterious. But such words can do no more than indicate and hint at something which is beyond description. Reality cannot be described; it can only be directly apprehended — that is, *realized*.

The outward forms of religion can but give an intimation. A church, for example, which is not only finely constructed and beautiful, but which also has an atmosphere of piety, may give such an intimation. In such a church we may experience that *otherness* which compels us to leave the things of the world outside, to become still, and to kneel down.

This is forcefully expressed in the passage of the burning bush: "And He said: 'Come not nigh hither, put off the shoes from thy feet: for the place whereon thou standest is holy ground.' "[11]

There are people who have something of that otherness. They shatter the complacency of one's habitual existence; they shift the emphasis of things and call up invocations of that which, in the last resort, alone is important. These are intimations of God's holiness, of that nature which is wholly His own — that unique and supremely precious essence of God whereon depends our all — our eternal welfare, our salvation.

Holiness means that God is pure, that He is of a mighty all-consuming purity which permits no blemish. It means that He is good, not in the sense merely that He has all those qualities which are encompassed by the concept *good*, but also in the sense that "none is good but one, that is God."[12] In short, God is the supreme good.

[11]Exod. 3:5.
[12]Mark 10:18.

That which we call *good* on earth can be likened to a splinter from the infinite bounty of His being. God is the standard by which all is measured, the ultimate test to which everything has to submit, the ultimate judgment over all and everything.

God's holiness makes prayer possible

As soon as man comes into the proximity of God, he is confronted by this holiness, becomes aware of it, and responds to it in various ways.

He becomes aware that he himself is not holy, that he is profane and earthly — indeed, that he is sinful and guilty. He realizes that he is not fit to be in the presence of God and wishes either to go away from Him, or to say with Peter, "Depart from me, for I am a sinful man, O Lord."[13]

Yet, at the same time, he knows that he stands in perpetual need of this holy God, that it is literally a matter of life or death to him, for he knows that he can live only through Him and that in the final analysis he can be nowhere else but with Him. Thus despite his own unworthiness, he is impelled toward God, impelled to speak in the words of the Psalm: "O God, my God, for Thee do I watch at break of day. For Thee my soul hath thirsted; for Thee my flesh, O how many ways! In a desert land, and where there is no way, and no water."[14]

From these two responses spring the forms of prayer. For ultimately prayer is man's answer to God's holiness. A God merely omniscient, all-just, omnipotent, and all-real, would be an enormity otherwise — the Absolute Being. We might admire Him, stand in awe of Him, feel overwhelmed by Him, but we could not

[13]Luke 5:8.
[14]Ps. 62:2-3 (RSV: Ps. 63:1).

pray to Him. It is God's holiness which makes prayer possible. It is only holiness which imbues God's omniscience, justice, and reality with those characteristics, and gives to it those powers of intimate contact which make prayer possible. One might almost say that the act of prayer expresses in man something of that nature, the supreme — the divine — expression of which is God's holiness.

God's holiness makes us uncomfortable

There is a third human reaction to God's holiness. It is an evil reaction; it rises from man's contradictory nature and consists of a feeling of discomfort, irritation, and rebelliousness. A strange manifestation! One is inclined to ask how this can come about if God is the moving Spirit and essence of the universe, and man is His creature — "For in Him we live, and move, and are."[15]

It is indeed difficult to understand; it springs from the mystery of evil. Sin, ultimately, is resistance to the holiness of God. It would be a mistake to think of this resistance merely as an open rebellion against, or as a denial of, God.

Potentially it is present in all of us — sometimes stronger, sometimes weaker; sometimes quite openly, sometimes in the guise of self-sufficient (rational) culture, or healthy common sense. When resistance, open or otherwise, gains the upper hand, prayer becomes impossible.

We must watch out for signs of it in ourselves; we must face it, try to resolve or still it, or overcome it with firm determination, whichever may be for us the most effective way of dealing with it. Let us leave this and return to the two fundamental motives of prayer already referred to.

[15]Acts 17:28.

Prayer's first motive: a sense of our own sinfulness

The first motive for prayer springs from man's awareness of his own unworthiness before the holiness of God. Man recognizes that he is selfish, unjust, deficient, and impure. He acknowledges his own wrongdoings and tries to assess them: not merely those of today or of yesterday, but of the whole of his life. Beyond this he tries to visualize the whole of the human condition with its shortcomings. He realizes sin as it is understood by the Scriptures, sin as it is active in himself. He recognizes that sin is transgression of the moral law and of the natural law.

But even more, he recognizes that sin is contumacy before God's holiness, that it is, therefore, not only wicked but unholy. He admits it and sides with God against himself; he says, in the words of the Psalm: "For I know my iniquity, and my sin is always before me. Against Thee only have I sinned, and have done evil before Thee: that Thou mayst be justified in Thy words, and mayst overcome when Thou art judged."[16]

We sometimes deny our own guilt

There are many ways in which man may try to evade this acknowledgment. The crudest form of evasion consists in a deliberate denial of his guilt. He considers himself pure, persuades himself that he has always been righteous and has committed no sin. He does not realize what presumption there is behind his pretense of righteousness, how much there is amiss behind his allegedly blameless conduct. What is required here is the will and the courage to face the truth. God has told us that we are sinners,

[16]Ps. 50:5-6 (RSV: Ps. 51:3-4).

and it is unbelief not to take it seriously. "If we say that we have no sin, we deceive ourselves, and the truth is not in us. If we confess our sins, He is faithful and just, to forgive us our sins, and to cleanse us from all iniquity. If we say that we have not sinned, we make Him a liar, and His word is not in us."[17] These words show how self-deceptive is the feeling of our purity and our righteousness. They clearly state our condition before God and point the path to true understanding.

It does not follow that we should torment ourselves over our sinful ways. This also would be acting against truth and, moreover, could become a form of self-indulgence, which might have evil consequences. Obsession with the thought of sinfulness has invariably led either the persons so obsessed — or a later generation — to some form of rebellion. Christian teaching about sin gives us a new understanding which encourages and enables us to strive for purer righteousness. The acknowledgment of our sins must not make us despondent and discouraged; on the contrary, it ought to call forth in us the desire for spiritual purification and renewal.

We sometimes wrongly consider sinfulness acceptable

There is another way of attempting to evade the issue: that is, by giving way to that false pride which prevents man from admitting to himself that he is a sinner, although he does not hide the fact that he has done wrong and is doing wrong. But since he cannot alter the fact he simply says, "My place is not with God," and turns away.

What is lacking here is humility. Man should be able not only to acknowledge that he is a sinner, but also to face the idea — not

[17]1 John 1:8-10.

in a spirit of defiance and self-assertiveness, but with sincerity and good-will; not in a spirit of self-abasement and mortification, but honorably and responsibly. In short, man must reconcile himself to the idea that he is a sinner and must learn to bear the stigma. This will open the way to self-renewal.

We sometimes despair

A third form of evasion is caused by lack of courage. When man sees that he is constantly transgressing and that evil is deeply rooted in him, when he begins to feel that all is confusion and that there is no way out, he runs the risk of despairing of himself, especially when he is a person wanting in willpower and, perhaps, in logic. To hold out in these circumstances is most difficult because the mind seems to answer to all good intentions, "You're not going to carry this through; you will do again what you have always done before." There is only one remedy: to put aside all inner searchings and recriminations, to have done with all hesitations, and to put one's absolute trust in God who "quickeneth the dead; and calleth those things that are not, as those that are."[18] From this act of surrender to the Absolute, above and within us, will spring new resolve and new strength. We shall be able to say, "I will and *shall*, for God the omnipotent *wills* it."

God's forgiveness makes repentance possible

There is another mysterious aspect of God's power which makes it possible for man to acknowledge his wrong and to admit and confess his sins. Man knows this intuitively, and the Scriptures

[18]Rom. 4:17.

have revealed it to us. God is not only the prime cause of the good and the fount of all justice; He is the all-renewer. He can give a new beginning to what appears final and He can undo all deeds. The words of St. Paul quoted above point to this mystery. God who is the supreme holiness, which by definition excludes all evil, is willing and able to forgive and to renew.

True forgiveness, the forgiveness which we are seeking and which alone is of benefit to us, is a great mystery. It implies not only that God decides to overlook what has happened and turns lovingly toward the sinner; this would not be sufficient. God's forgiveness is creative: it makes him who has become guilty free of all guilt. God gathers the guilty man into His holiness, makes him partake of it, and gives him a new beginning. It is to this mystery that man appeals when he acknowledges his sins, repents of them, and seeks forgiveness. This is the first of those two motives of prayer which come into being before God's holiness.

Prayer's second motive: the yearning for union

The second motive for prayer begins with the recognition that, despite our resistance to God, we cannot be without Him. The first motive expresses what Peter said to Christ when he felt His mysterious powers by the lake of Genesareth: "Depart from me, for I am a sinful man, O Lord."[19] The second finds its expression once again in the words of Peter at Capharnaum, when our Lord promised the Eucharist: "Lord, to whom shall we go? Thou hast the words of eternal life. And we have believed and have known, that thou art the Christ, the Son of God."[20]

[19]Luke 5:8.
[20]John 6:69-70.

If the knowledge of our sinfulness leads us either to arrogance or dejection, the link between God and man breaks and we turn away from Him. But if it leads us to humility and truth, then we may say, "It is true that by my sins I have forfeited the right of being in the presence of God, but where else shall I be if I cannot be with Him?"

God's holiness calls us to Him

The same holiness which turns man away also recalls him, for holiness is love. It rejects man so that he may find true humility and the new way. When he has done this — however insufficiently — it calls him anew.

We know that God is the supreme good, the supreme being, salvation — life. That is why we yearn for God. If we do not have this yearning — life may have disheartened or disillusioned us or made us dull and indifferent — we must endeavor to awaken it through faith. We must guard against that attitude of spiritual pride which makes us say, "What I do not feel I do not need." We must allow for the possibility that our feelings may be unreliable and therefore we must honestly strive to correct them. Yearning for God is inborn in human nature. If it is lacking, it does not follow that we have no need of God, but rather that we may be sick and in need of healing. It may be humiliating to have to admit to oneself that one is lacking something which is an intrinsic part of human nature. It may easily lead one to adopt an attitude of defiance, which, although giving an impression of superiority, is in fact rather pathetic.

We said previously that even if we do not directly apprehend God's reality we must accept it as a fundamental tenet of our faith. In the same way, we must have recourse to faith if our own feelings do not prompt us to seek God. This is the truth — all else is error.

The yearning for God is a form of prayer

This yearning for God — a yearning for union, for participation — is also prayer. The story is told of St. Thomas Aquinas that when he had finished an important section of his great work on divine truth, Christ appeared to him and said, "Thou hast written well about me, Thomas. What shall I give thee?" St. Thomas, the legend goes, answered, "Thyself, Lord." St. Teresa expressed this yearning even more forcefully when she wrote: "Only God is sufficient."[21]

The deepest core, the highest aspirations, the whole essence and purpose of man's striving can be summed up in the proposition: man's soul longs for union with God. This is not merely the expression of a pious sentiment; it is the precise truth.

We want to possess that which we consider to be precious and real. But is there anything in the world which we are really able to possess? Something catches our fancy, we buy it, we take it and carry it home, but do we really possess it? It is true we can make use of it; we can prevent anyone else having it, but is it ever truly ours? Not only may we lose it, not only can it be ruined, not only shall we have to give it up one day — we never really *have* it; we only hold it externally. We are never able to form that innermost union between ourselves and things which alone can be called *having*; there always remains a gulf.

The same applies to human relations. We want to establish a close relationship — a true union — with another person. We want to be certain of the other person, but can we ever achieve this? We may gain a person's confidence or love; we may be linked to that person by the strongest bonds of loyalty and devotion, but

[21]St. Teresa of Avila, Poem 9, "*Nada te turbe*."

ultimately that person still remains distant and inaccessible. God alone, the all-true, the all-being, the Holy, the Remote, is able to give Himself fully to man. Neither things nor persons, nor even we ourselves can fully become our own: only God can create that nearness that fulfills our yearning.

Again and again the cry "My God" appears in the Scriptures. "I said to the Lord: 'Thou art my God.' "[22] This is the heart's own cry, called forth by God Himself, who spoke thus: "I will walk among you, and will be your God."[23]

St. Augustine describes the nature of the human soul by saying that it is "capable of comprehending God." Capable — and this is even more important — of comprehending nothing but God and therefore, we may add, capable of comprehending the world and people only through God.

This finds expression in the prayer in which we strive for God, strive to partake of His plenitude, strive to be at one with Him. In this striving, prayer becomes love, for love means seeking to be completely at one with another autonomous being. We may acquire a jewel, a flower, or a work of art, and, to the extent to which we are able to establish an inner relationship with one of these objects, we may claim them as our own. But we cannot claim a human being as our own unless the right has been granted to us by that human being, unless he has permitted it of his own accord.

How, then, can God become our own? That He, who is Lord of Himself and of all creation, wishes to give Himself to us, and that it is compatible with His divinity to do so, only He Himself can reveal to us. Moreover, He must give us faith so that we may believe it and consummate the union.

[22] Ps. 139:7 (RSV: Ps. 140:6).
[23] Lev. 26:12.

48

This is the mystery of divine love, that in it all love has its origin and finds its complete fulfillment. We must therefore beseech God for the grace of His love and for grace to respond to it.

These two elements — the turning away from God, conscious that we are unworthy of Him, and the striving after Him in the longing for union — are to some degree present in every prayer which deserves the name. By these two contradictory trends we testify to God's holiness, for it is God's holiness which makes us shrink back in the knowledge that we ourselves are unholy, but which at the same time makes us strive after Him in the knowledge that in Him lies our salvation.

God is almighty

Another aspect of the nature of God, which we apprehend in some forms of religious experience, is His almighty power. The Scriptures abound in testimonies to the majesty and power of God. Frequently these testamonies are in the form of statements about the greatness of the world, which is then said to be nothing in comparison with God.

The Old Testament opens with the great hymn of the creation of the world. Its realms unfold before our eyes, each one issuing forth from the Word of God. The world is through Him; He is of Himself. Heaven and earth, darkness and light, the waters and the land, are what He commands them to be; He, however, is one and everything. There is no primary matter, no plan; everything comes into being through Him alone.

He is not only greater than the world, but absolute greatness — greatness in itself. The world, however, is only through Him and before His sight.

This greatness is free; it is the first source of all order. God utters the words "Let there be," and everything becomes.

However, when God's greatness encounters man's defiance, His greatness becomes inexorable and changes into the wrath of God, of which the destructive powers of nature, such as storms, earthquakes, the scorching sun, and the tumultuous seas are warning manifestations.[24]

Providence reveals God's loving power

Yet God's awfulness is all kindness, wisdom, and tenderness, for does not God teach His prophet that the Lord is not in the wind, the earthquake, or the fire, but in the whistling of a gentle air?[25]

It is in the doctrine of divine Providence that the almighty power of God fully reveals itself to us. In this doctrine, the awfulness of omniscience, the ineffableness of omnipotence, and the unfathomableness of a wisdom which controls the immeasurable threads of existence declare themselves as pure love: in Providence God the Almighty becomes the Father.

God is infinite

Human existence is finite in every respect: we are limited in our physical size, in our possessions, in the space we inhabit. Everyone has his own particular disposition and temperament, which is the measure both of his possibilities and of his limitations. Again and again — in being and in having, in our relations to things and people — we learn this lesson: *so far and no farther*. It is different with God. He knows no restriction or limitation, for He is and has everything: He is the all-embracing, the infinite.

[24]Pss. 75, 96 (RSV: Pss. 76, 97).
[25]3 Kings 19:11-12 (RSV: 1 Kings 19:11-12).

God's being is inexhaustible in substance. From unfathomable depths it rises and then extends over measureless space. The greatest heights which we are able to conceive can be but a pale intimation of His sublimity.

Our power is as limited as our being. In all our endeavors, struggles, and activities we inevitably reach the point beyond which, we realize, we cannot go: the point which marks the frontier of our knowledge and of our faculties.

God knows no such limitations. He creates, and in the most perfect way: by the Word alone. All that has been given to us — the world in all its abundance of forms, its diversity of laws, the immeasurableness of all things great and small — all this issued forth from the Word of God.

God is the ultimate good

Yet all that has been said so far does not do justice to the greatness of God. The attribute *great* does not merely denote a high degree of being and of power; it also denotes a high degree of value — it denotes excellence of quality. Thus we would call *great* a man possessing great purity of heart and nobility of mind; we would also call *great* a work of man if it expressed purity and noble intent. By this token, a painting twelve inches square, if it expressed these qualities, would be *greater* than one which covered the wall but did not express them.

God is not only the all-real, but also the all-good. When we pronounce the word *truth* we thereby express that all-embracing plenitude of pure integrity of essence which is God. Again, when we speak of *justice, purity, harmony* — these are really ways of referring to Him. *Beauty* is not really an attribute but a proper name of God. It is value — goodness, truth, beauty — from which all that is derives its ultimate right *to be*.

God not only demands value, and imposes value but is the form (or idea) of value. More than that: God is the supreme Universal — the universal of universals — of which all particulars, including all values, are mere reflections.

Thus His reality is absolutely justified and necessary. He alone has substance and the sovereign right *to be*.

Mere existence is dark and brooding; value gives it light. "This is the declaration which we have heard from Him and declare unto you: that God is light, and in Him there is no darkness."[26]

God's mighty power, as we have pointed out, is all tenderness and love, capable of giving everything and of giving itself.

Finally, life is more than breathing, growing, working, creating, and experiencing. Life is — or should be — self-experiencing and, ultimately, *self-realization*. How much there is in us which we do not realize, which, indeed, seems unrealizable!

God is omniscient. His omniscience embraces the world and mankind; but, above all, it is directed toward Himself. God is self-realized in the fullness of His infinite being. Aware of His own majesty, He carries the inconceivable momentousness of His own being in the supreme freedom of His will.

These reflections can do no more than give an intimation of God's greatness: a greatness which is beyond all measure, yet is not inordinate or unwieldy, but light, luminous, and controlled — in short, perfect.

Adoration is the proper response to God's goodness

Before this greatness man inclines himself, not only in the literal sense but in the devotion of his heart. He inclines himself

---

[26]1 John 1:5.

without reservation, in complete surrender as the creature before the Creator: in short, he adores. The act of adoration expresses the realization that God is greatness, pure and simple, and that man is smallness, pure and simple; that God exists by reason of Himself and in Himself, but man only through God and by God's grace.

Adoration affirms: "Thou art God; I am man. Thou art the One that truly is, self-created, substantial from all eternity. I am only through Thee and in Thy sight. Thou hast all plenitude of being, all fullness of value, all sublimity of meaning; Thou art Lord and unto Thyself. The meaning of my existence, however, is derived from Thine. I live in Thy light and the measure of my existence is in Thee."

God is worthy of our adoration

It is important to stress that in this act of worship man does not submit to God simply because God is so infinitely greater than man. If this were the only reason for man's submission it would mean that God's almighty power had left him no choice but to yield. Man submits because he knows that this is right and just in itself. If adoration merely expressed "I submit to Thee because Thou art stronger than I," this would be a feeble and ultimately unworthy sentiment. But adoration says: "I submit because Thou art worthy of this act of homage. I have apprehended that Thou art not only *reality* but *truth*; not only *power* but also *goodness*; not only *dominion* but *infinite merit* and the meaning of meaning."

In the life of man, might and right, strength and merit, actuality and truth, status and worthiness rarely coincide; it is this which makes our existence so drifting and questionable. It demands from us constant striving, and at the same time fills us with a sense of futility. With God it is different. Whenever man encounters God he finds in His might also right, in His greatness also worthiness.

There is no dichotomy in God's nature; with Him being and action are one. To all this we give expression in adoration.

A God merely all-real and omnipotent, man could not adore. He could not resist such a God; he would have to surrender unconditionally to Him. For the sake, however, of his dignity as a person, he would have to deny Him adoration. In the act of adoration it is not only the body which is bowed down, but the person as a whole, and this can be done only voluntarily and with dignity. The unity of being and meaning in God renders this possible. This is magnificently illustrated in the book of Revelation in the passage of the four-and-twenty elders (the last representatives of the human race) worshipping Him and casting their crowns before Him, saying: "Thou art worthy, O Lord our God, to receive glory, and honor, and power: because Thou hast created all things; and for Thy will they were, and have been created."[27]

Adoration is more important than petition

Apart from the special importance which attaches to the act of adoration as an integral part of religious worship, it is important also as an element in man's spiritual life as a whole. It is as necessary to man's spiritual existence as the laws of logic are to his intellectual life or the spatial order is to his physical existence. Or, using a different analogy, we may say that adoration is to man's spiritual vision what light is to his physical eye.

Human existence is founded in truth, and the foundation of all truth is that God is God — unique, alone, and unto Himself; and that man is God's creature. By recognizing this fundamental truth and by acting in accordance with it man maintains his integrity

[27]Rev. 4:11.

and his wholeness. Adoration is the act in which this truth continually rises resplendent, and in which it is acknowledged and consummated.

It is important that we practice adoration because normally we tend in our prayers to put too much emphasis on asking. Of course we should ask, but let us not forget what Christ said in the Sermon on the Mount: "For your Father knoweth what is needful for you, before you ask Him."[28] More important than petition is adoration, for in it truth will come to us — the truth of life. Everyday cares will find their proper place and our standards will become rightly adjusted. This truth will comfort us; it will put in order what the entanglements and illusions of life have thrown into confusion. It will heal us spiritually so that we may begin anew.

God is worthy of praise

The greatness of God is expressed in the very names by which we call Him. He is the *Uncreated*, who has made everything; the One without beginning who is self-sustained; the *Infinite*; the *Immortal*; the *Eternal*. Because He is master of Himself, Lord of His own divinity, He is the Master and Lord of all that is. Thus the universe is His by dominion and by right.

Man inclines himself in adoration before Him completely and unconditionally, in freedom and dignity. In the Scriptures, God's greatness and His majesty are experienced also as splendor and glory, terms which convey the all-penetrating radiance — the effulgence of the Divine Reality — before which adoration assumes the character of praise and jubilation. Thus the Scriptures contain passage after passage proclaiming the splendor of God,

[28]Matt. 6:8.

singing His praise, extolling His holiness, majesty, might, eternity, infinite freedom, justice, goodness, mercy, and patience.

One might object that there is something embarrassing about such fulsomeness; that it savors of the submissiveness of the weak, of the sycophancy of the defenseless, which is contrary to the dignity of man and even more so to the dignity of God.

No doubt, when the motives are not absolutely pure, praise — especially the praise of God — deserves this criticism. But when the motives are pure, bestowing praise is perfectly consistent with dignity and honor. One may, for example, have occasion to commend a person for his reliability. Ought one to refrain from it for fear of being thought a flatterer? Indeed, it may sometimes be a real act of friendship to let a person know how highly we think of him and how much we rely upon him. To convey to a person spontaneously and gladly what we find attractive or praiseworthy about him is not flattery but a form of praise which makes for the beauty of human relations.

God certainly does not need our assurance that we value His lofty qualities, yet it is "meet and just" and a form of the purest and truest prayer when man rejoices in God and glorifies Him. The Scriptures, as has been noted, abound in songs of praise. Among the Psalms there are many which, springing from man's profound experience of the glory of God, pour forth holy emotion in praising His qualities and His works one by one.[29] In the Prophets also, praise of the Lord breaks through again and again, to give as an example only the great song of praise of the Seraphim in Isaiah's vision: "And they cried one to another, and said: 'Holy, holy, holy, the Lord God of Hosts, all the earth is full of His glory.' "[30]

[29]Psalms 32, 46, 95, and 99 should be given special mention (RSV: Pss. 33, 47, 96, and 100).

[30]Isa. 6:3.

In the New Testament we find the *Magnificat*[31] and the song of Zachariah.[32] The Liturgy, too, is permeated by songs of praise such as the *Te Deum* and many hymns and sequences.

Sometimes it is as though the praise of God filled the world; as if it went out to and enfolded all creation, as for instance the Psalms of creation[33] or in the response which those songs have found in the hearts of God-enraptured people such as St. Francis of Assisi. In the last of the Psalms mentioned above, creation and creatures are exhorted to praise God:

> *Praise ye the Lord from the heavens:*
> *praise ye Him in the high places.*
> *Praise ye Him, all His angels:*
> *praise ye Him, all His hosts.*
> *Praise ye Him, O sun and moon:*
> *praise Him, all ye stars and light.*
> *Praise Him, ye heavens of heavens:*
> *and let all the waters that are above the heavens*
> *Praise the name of the Lord.*
>
> *For He spoke,*
> *and they were made:*
> *He commanded,*
> *and they were created.*
> *He hath established them for ever,*
> *and for ages of ages:*
> *He hath made a decree,*
> *and it shall not pass away.*

[31]Luke 1:46-55.
[32]Luke 1:68-79.
[33]Pss. 18, 103, 104, and 148 (RSV: Pss. 19, 104, 105, and 148).

Praise the Lord from the earth,
 ye dragons, and all ye deeps:
Fire, hail, snow, ice, stormy winds,
 which fulfill His word:
Mountains and all hills,
 fruitful trees and all cedars:
Beasts and all cattle:
 serpents and feathered fowls.[34]

This is not a fairy-tale approach to nature in which the sun and the moon, the trees, and so forth are personalized and given voices with which to sing the praise of God; it is an inspired poetic rendering of the idea that the sun and the moon and all created things are a mirror of God's glory because, as His creation, they reflect something of His nature. In so doing, they praise Him by their very existence. They themselves know nothing of it, but man does; he can think himself into their silent song of praise; he can voice it on their behalf, offer it up to God and thus act as the spokesman of creation.

When discussing adoration we said that man humbles himself before God, not because God is all-powerful, but because He is truth and goodness and worthy of adoration. In other words, God proves — if one may express it thus — His divinity by His character. With Him, being and doing are one; essence and existence are one; promise and fulfillment are one. From this derives the ultimate justification of praise.

"Lord, Thou art almighty" is synonymous with "Lord, Thou art worthy of being almighty; Thou livest Thy almightiness — with Thy character and acts. Thy almightiness is the supreme consummation of justice and truth." It is therefore fitting to praise God.

---

[34]Ps. 148:1-10 (RSV: Ps. 148: 1-10).

Man's spirit rejoices that God *is that He is*. This joy pours forth in praise. The attributes of God which man is able to name are merely like so many rays of that effulgent light, like so many emanations of that arch-unity of being and necessity that is His inmost essence which cannot be named, in short, like so many emanations of the *Who Am* ("God said to Moses: '*I Am Who Am.*' ")[35]

It is *Who Am* which enkindles in man the flame of gladness which turns to gratitude and finds expression in praise. We praise God and give thanks to Him for the glorious reality of His *being*. In the words of the *Gloria:* "We give thanks for Thy great glory, O Lord God, heavenly king, God the Father." And in the words of the *Preface:* "It is truly meet and just that we should always, and in all places give thanks to Thee, all-holy Lord, Father Almighty, Eternal God."

Praise elevates the person praising

The praise is the purer, the more profound the experience of God's glory and the truer the joy to which it gives rise. In praise, man himself becomes pure and great, for his greatness derives not only from what he is in himself, but from his ability to value and honor that which is greater than himself.

Therefore, it is "meet and just" to do homage to Him who is the supreme greatness and glory; at the same time this act of homage is an act of self-realization for him who performs it. Man's real world is, as it were, above him. Praising God means ascending into that homeland of our spirit where, it may be said, we truly live.

Thus we should practice giving praise to God. This discipline widens and edifies the spirit. The whole day assumes a different

[35]Exod. 3:14.

character if, on waking in the morning, rested and refreshed from the night, we recite the words of the *Te Deum* or of the 148th Psalm. There are no morning prayers more beautiful than these.

Certainly it is right for us to *ask* in prayer and to put before God the problems of our burdensome existence. Yet it might profit us more if we directed our gaze away from ourselves toward Him. Our cares and needs would not be forgotten for, in Christ's words, "Your Father knoweth what is needful for you, before you ask Him."[36]

The loving God is generous and bountiful

God's being is inexhaustible. Ever new aspects of His being reveal themselves to us in contemplation and religious experience, and to every one of them our souls can respond in prayer. Thus theology itself almost becomes a school for prayer.

This book is merely an introduction; we shall therefore confine ourselves here to considering a final group of divine attributes to which we make direct appeal in our prayers: God is bountiful and generous. He cares for man; He values and loves him. Two forms of prayer in particular — petition and thanksgiving — go out to these aspects of God.

God loves us

Some conceptions of the Deity preclude all possibility of either petition or thanksgiving (for example, that God is merely the First Cause — the unmoved mover of the universe — or the idea of the good). To such a god the heart of man could not turn when in distress. In his sight, petition would be as futile as gratitude; awe

[36]Matt. 6:8.

and admiration would be the only possible reaction to a god conceived in this way.

However, the Scriptures tell us that God is *vis viva;* that He is the power of willing and of action; that He is Person, able to listen and respond.

God is *spirit,* not in the impersonal sense of an intellectual principle in which the word is often understood, but in the sense given to it by the Scriptures when they refer to Him as the "living God."

God is the creative, the inexhaustible, the ever close and benevolent One. He is also the "rich" God, as the spiritual masters put it, who is willing to share the abundance of His being with us. He is the ever giving, who can never suffer diminution by His gifts; who never tires in His generosity; who can never be disappointed, for He does not depend on the response of those to whom He gives. He gives creatively. To such a god the heart of man can turn.

Our God does not dwell in Olympian heights, in blissful self-sufficiency, indifferent to the plight of human existence. If this were so, prayer would be of no avail; indeed, it would be undignified and hopeless from the start. The Scriptures tell us that God is concerned with man and that He loves him. God's love for man is the main theme of the Gospel and the whole of Christ's life proclaims it. This is true Revelation — that is, something which the mind of man could not have grasped on its own.

This love, so revealed, means not only that God wishes His creatures well but that He truly loves them with an earnestness to which the Incarnation bears witness. It means that God has given Himself in this love, making it — if we may thus express it — His destiny.

This love prepares the ground for its ultimate self-revelation by the creation of the world; its design becomes more distinct in the course of the sacred history which leads up to Christ. In His life and His teaching it comes out into the open, to spread in the pattern of Divine Providence through space and time to its final consummation in the new creation and in the coming of the kingdom of God.

A profound mystery surrounds the origin of divine love, so that to the question as to why God loves man, man himself cannot give an answer. God's love must be regarded as pure gift, as the creative cause of itself.

There is another aspect to this love, which must be understood in order to get a balanced picture. God's love for man must be worthy of God Himself: this it can be only if it is worthy of man as a person. Having invested man with the dignity of free will and responsibility, God treats him in a manner befitting this status; in other words, He honors man. This does not imply that man possesses anything in his own right which would compel God's respect, for whatever man possesses, including his status as a person, God has given to him. But having given it to him, God treats him accordingly. For the sake of His own honor, God maintains the dignity of man.

This must be strongly emphasized, for there is a manner of interpreting the sovereign, absolute status of God which consists in contrasting it with the contingent, doubtful status of man. This interpretation does not serve the glory either of God or of His creature, for one does not honor God by degrading man.

It is true that man is but a creature, and a fallen, erring one at that. But he is not mere nothingness or sheer demerit; he has significance in the sight of God when God loves him.

Prayers of petition

To this God we lift up our hearts in prayer. We turn to Him, the omnipotent being, of whose love we feel certain, as the child in distress turns to his mother or as we turn to a friend when we need comfort or help. Christ taught us that we should turn to the Father and ask Him to "give us this day our daily bread" — meaning the necessities of our daily life. He admonished us to do it simply and trustingly, because "your Father knoweth what is needful for you, before you ask Him."[37]

Christ teaches us to ask for assistance

How simple and natural is this asking we know from the incident related in the eleventh chapter in the Gospel according to St. Luke. There the disciples come to the Master asking Him to teach them to pray. He teaches them the Lord's Prayer, which is one long petition. It encompasses the whole of our existence, acknowledges its dependence on God, and receives it from His hand.

We are taught to pray for everything: for the necessities of life, for strength in our labors, for comfort in spiritual distress, for support in our moral struggles, for the understanding of truth, for greater charity and righteousness. Man is ever conscious of his want and helplessness; it is only right, therefore, that he should turn to the bountiful and almighty God, who is not only ready to give and to help, but greatly rejoices in it.

Prayers of petition acknowledge God's bountifulness

Asking for help means more than turning to God only when we have reached the end of our resources. His help does more than merely fill the gaps in our own ability. Therefore, what we ask for

[37]Matt. 6:8.

in prayer is, strictly speaking, not help in the sense of something additional or supplementary to what we have — our whole life is founded in God. Everything we do comes to us from Him and goes out to Him. There is no such thing as a complete, self-sufficient human being, a human being at his own risk and responsibility. To be man is to have one's being *from* and *in* God. This fact is constantly stressed in the Scriptures.

Prayer, therefore, is not really a call for help but the acknowledgment of the fact that man receives substance and existence, life and meaning, freedom and strength, through God's creative dispensation — that he exists by the grace of God. All this may be called grace in a wider sense, because he receives as a free favor what he can neither claim nor enforce.

Grace in the strict meaning of the term is everything that comes to us by God's redeeming love in the form of light, strength, guidance, spiritual comfort, and liberation. Thus all petition in prayer is ultimately petition for grace in the wider as well as the more precise meaning of the term. This prayer for grace must be constantly renewed, since at every instant we have our being by the grace of God. Prayer for grace is as essential to life as breath.

We must pray for others

Petition must not forget our fellow men. The believer must include in his thoughts those whom he loves and for whom he is responsible. God knows of them and loves them with greater purity and power than any human being (even the most loving) is capable of doing. God has the power to protect them, to help them, and to bless them.

It is right that we should think in our prayers of those who are dear to us, dwell lovingly on their problems and cares, and bring these before God. It is comforting to share one's concern over a person dear to us with the all-providing God and to be able to say to oneself that he is safe in God's care. It gives peace and confidence; it frees us temporarily from anxiety and torment; and, even if they should return later, the relief which prayer afforded us cannot be undone.

We should also take before God everything that concerns the community as a whole: the events of current history, the needs of the people, the sorrows of the age. Everyone is responsible for the whole of human existence. Although the powers of the individual are, on the whole, very limited, in prayer everyone is able to encompass everything and to take it to Him who guides the destiny of the world. God does not compel man; He has made him free and guides him only through freedom. The door to freedom opens in two aspects of our existence: when we act and when in our prayers we place before God the common cause of mankind.

Prayer is necessary when faith feels disappointed

We said that man turns to God for succor and comfort by inner necessity and with the same spontaneity and artlessness with which a child turns to his mother. However, it may not always be so. It may happen that we find it difficult, even impossible, to ask anything of God and therefore have to learn anew how to do it. Life brings many disappointments. It may happen that we have prayed in an hour of distress and our prayer has remained unanswered. We may have felt lost and sought God but not found Him.

There may be other reasons: as we grow older many of us also become hardened, relying on our own strength to cope as best we can with the problems of life. This attitude does not favor prayer; it may even make prayer appear childish and futile. If this happens we must strengthen our faith to overrule our feeling. We must seek reassurance in God's word as revealed to us in the Scriptures and pray in the assurance of His love, even though we may not feel it. If, then, we persevere, our prayers will be heard, even though what we ask for may be granted in a way different from what we had anticipated.

Prayer is necessary when faith is weak

Then, again, we may have the feeling that God is indifferent and is not concerned with mankind; that He dwells in remote spheres while man is delivered up to the hopeless predicament of earthly existence. Such thoughts come readily to people who have gone through much sorrow: to the sad, the silent, and the harassed — and to those who are unable to take things lightly and for whom everything seems to turn out for the worst.

Such people stand in great need of human love and understanding, if only to convince them that things are not as bad as they themselves think. In the absence of such love and such understanding, they must hold on to the faith which tells them that God loves them and they must try again and again to turn to Him in prayer.

Then, again, it may happen that we are unable to conceive of God as a living reality. He appears to us as a pious thought, a holy mood — something beautiful but far away and ephemeral which has no place in the actuality of life. It is not easy to counteract this kind of feeling or mood and to convince oneself that God is a reality, a greater reality than the familiar world. This understanding cannot be gained by the mind alone but only with the wholeness of our being; for the mind is an instrument which may become blunt and our capacity of feeling may be dulled. We must tell ourselves that the reality of God is of a very exalted and special kind and that, in order to experience it, we must be able to go beyond thought and feeling.

Yet the reality of God is not one which is opposed to the reality of the world which He has created. The familiar world which surrounds us obtains its meaning as an intelligible whole from God. God does not, so to speak, flaunt His reality at the expense of the world. He leaves it to man to recognize it in the things of the world — as it were *behind* them, *above* them, and *beyond* them. Man has the faculty to do this, if he but has the right resolve.

Or it may happen that, confronted with the inexorability of life, we reach the conclusion that God has no power over the world, and that everything happens as it must inevitably happen in accordance with the immutable laws of nature.

Every cause has its effect and every effect in turn becomes a cause. In our own life outward circumstances, inner disposition, and everything that has gone before produce their effect. In all this — in this unbroken chain of causation — there seems little scope for a creative, giving, and helping Deity. This would seem to make prayer for divine intervention an absurdity. Again we must try to probe more deeply; we must try to understand that knowledge, empirically gained, has its validity, but that this validity is limited. As we grow up, understanding gained by observation replaces the more naïve beliefs of childhood.

It is quite proper that this should be so, for we have to come to terms with the actuality of life. However, this adult view of life may become destructive if it becomes too rigid, shutting man off from the wholeness of life. Life with all its laws — to which empirical knowledge can give but limited access — lies in the hand of God and can therefore be experienced only in a living relationship between God and man.

If man exercises his privilege of free will and makes the move toward God, he will find that here is the point of growth from which the world may develop and change. For the world as man perceives it is not something which is final and complete. It evolves and completes itself from within man; and for everyone it changes in accordance with his understanding, disposition, and actions. Here, then, man may experience the working of divine government, and may find that prayer (together with faith and obedience) is a means by which he maintains that relationship with God which awakens and keeps alive deeper understanding.

In common experience it is the things and events of the world which appear to be real and effective. To counteract this erroneous notion, we must meditate upon the eternal, timeless reality of God, through whom everything exists. We must dwell upon the ways of God and say to ourselves that He does not work as man does with his tools, but in a thousand mysterious, subtle, and hidden ways through the very essence of things which are His servants. The place where God's governance is directly experienced is the inmost heart of man: in man's free will and in his capacity for love.

Wrong attitudes interfere with prayer

Arrogance — which consists in wanting to rely entirely on one's own power — may close the door to prayer; so also may hurt pride or shame. A proud person does not want to humble himself by supplication; he should know that spiritual pride hardens the heart and deludes the mind.

We exist by the grace of God; to admit this and to act accordingly is both truth and humility. This is the lesson the proud must learn. They must also learn that their conception of God is wrong, for they forget that God honors man.

A great deal of harm has been done by a mistaken kind of piety which believes that by degrading man we render honor to God. When this kind of piety speaks of the *mercy of God*, the term carries the implication of a rich man throwing crumbs to a beggar.

The terms *love*, *charity*, *grace*, and *help* are cheapened by a suggestion of condescension on the part of God toward man which must cause offense to any upright person.

Such an interpretation is very wide of the mark. Man is not contemptible. It is true that he has sinned — and what this means we can learn from the history of mankind and also by trying to visualize what Christ suffered for our sins.

Yet the dignity which the Creator has bestowed on man is thereby not extinguished. It is his very *dignity* which is the measure of man's guilt. Thus everything which comes from God to man contains, as its inmost core, respect; and everything which goes from man to God must contain that which God's respect has conferred on man — namely, dignity. For this reason, praying to God for help can be done in all dignity, as the granting of our wishes is done with honor.

We must ask that God's will may be done

Our prayer should never cease to go out to God, not only as a call in distress but as a constant appeal to His creative might and sanctifying grace.

That is why all prayer must carry by implication the words "Not as I will, but as thou wilt."[38] We do not know whether what we ask for when we are in distress is good for us. Nor do we know whether the shape we want to give to events in a particular situation will really lead to the proper solution. Our life does not obey the laws which govern business or professional work, where plans are drawn up and put into effect — more or less successfully as the case may be. Only a small part of what happens in our life results from what

[38]Matt. 26:39.

69

we see and understand; the other, and greater part, comes from unseen realms. It is to the unseen — the mystery of God — that we must direct our prayers; and we must be prepared to receive what is right in the eyes of God.

Moreover, we must not forget that every request is the expression of our will: not only of the rightful and righteous will for existence and life, for fulfillment and expansion, but also the self-seeking, selfish side of that will which puts one's own existence into the center of all things and tries to subject everything to its own ends.

This self-assertiveness is contained in our prayers. If, therefore, we expect our prayers to be granted by the Most Holy, we must be prepared to submit them to His judgment, and also prepared for Him to reject or change them. "Thy will be done" must be the core of all prayer, not only because the divine will is irresistible and inescapable, but because it is just and holy and contains within itself everything that is worthy of being.

Finally, in the realm to which we direct our prayer reigns not only supreme justice, power, and order, but also the love of the living God. This love He bestowed on us in absolute freedom. In our prayers we take our needs and wishes to God, beseeching Him to act in accordance with the sovereign decisions of His love. The sentence "Not as I will, but as Thou wilt," ultimately means "may Thy love prevail."

Thanksgiving is due to God unceasingly

As soon as prayer is answered it becomes thanksgiving. It comes naturally from the heart; it is man's response to God's grace. We should give thanks not only when a wish has been granted but at all times. Unceasingly the heart of man should respond to the dispensations of Divine Providence. This response consists in man being aware that everything he is and everything that happens to him comes from God and that he should acknowledge and be thankful for it.

The Apostle Paul says: "And be ye thankful . . . singing in grace in your hearts to God. All whatsoever you do in word or in work, do all in the name of the Lord Jesus Christ, giving thanks to God and the Father by Him."[39]

The seriousness of the offense of forgetting to give thanks is brought out in the story of the ten lepers, of whom only one, a Samaritan, returned to give thanks.

> And it came to pass, as He was going to Jerusalem, He passed through the midst of Samaria and Galilee. And as He entered into a certain town, there met Him ten men that were lepers, who stood afar off; and lifted up their voice, saying: "Jesus, master, have mercy on us." Whom when He saw, He said: "Go, shew yourselves to the priests." And it came to pass, as they went, they were made clean. And one of them, when he saw that he was made clean, went back, with a loud voice glorifying God. And he fell on his face before His feet, giving thanks: and this was a Samaritan. And Jesus answering, said: "Were not ten made clean? And where are the nine? There is no one found to return and give glory to God, but this stranger." And he said to him: "Arise, go thy way; for thy faith hath made thee whole."[40]

This is a cry of sorrow from the divine heart, similar to the one so often uttered through the mouth of the prophets when the people forgot to give thanks to the Lord who had bestowed so much on them.

[39]Col. 3:15-17.
[40]Luke 17:11-19.

71

Gratitude is due for gifts freely given

For things which happen by necessity we cannot give thanks. If we know the laws of nature and infer that certain causes will produce certain effects, we cannot feel gratitude, however beneficent these effects may be for us: they were bound to happen. In the same manner, we cannot experience true gratitude when we have sold some goods and received the correct payment for them. We receive this payment by right. Only when we receive something freely, without necessity or legal obligation on the part of the giver, do we spontaneously experience that intimate feeling which we express in the words "I thank you."

Existence must not be taken for granted

It is important that we should recognize — not only with our mind but with our heart — that nothing in life can be taken for granted. In a restricted sense, as we have just seen, certain natural events must be taken for granted, but this is true only when seen from a standpoint which does not take in life as a whole. We live in the world from which we draw the substances and energies to sustain our existence; we are linked to it by innumerable threads of cause and effect.

We therefore take it for granted, never stopping to think that it might well be otherwise, that this world, which appears to us the basis of everything, might not exist. It is an irreligious attitude to take the world for granted. Although in fact it does exist, there is no reason why it should. The world is not necessary; it exists because God willed it. At this point, there is no causation, only pure sovereign freedom.

The world has emerged out of the freedom of God, and His freedom is love; because it is love we can respond to it by gratitude.

It is therefore meet, just, and appropriate to give thanks to God for having created the world.

Nor ought I, as an individual, regard it as a matter of course that I should exist. I happen to find myself in this world, and in this body and mind of mine. In consequence, I take myself and my existence for granted, more so even than that of the world. It appears to me the precondition for everything else. Yet I know that I might equally well not exist. *To take a thing for granted* means "to accept it as a given fact."

Things exist only by God's grace

There is a deep double meaning in "to accept it as a given fact." On the one hand, it stands for "that which happens to be there" and is, by virtue of it, the precondition for everything else; on the other hand, it acknowledges in the word *given* that it is *there* neither by necessity nor by right, but *by grace*.

It is therefore proper that I should know and acknowledge in my heart that I constantly receive myself as a free gift from the hand of God. By the word *grace* we usually mean everything we receive from God by way of help, enlightenment, and sanctification, as opposed to those things — good or bad — that arise out of the potentialities inherent in conditions and people. Thus we oppose the concept *grace* to the concept *nature*. However, we can use the term *grace* in a much wider sense to include the origin of everything which does not exist by necessity but as God's free gift.

Thanksgiving is due for all of creation

This term includes the world as a whole, humanity, myself — in fact everything which exists except God Himself. Everything we take for granted is truly *granted* by Him, the all-giving.

There are moments when we suddenly and directly apprehend the incomprehensible, overwhelming fact that *we are*. Despite the tribulations and burdens of life it still remains a great grace and wonder that we are allowed to breathe, to feel, to think, to love, and to act — in short, to live. And that things exist: the jug on the table, the tree in the field, the landscape around us, and the sun in the sky; and that other people also exist: this person whom I love, that other one who is in my care. In those moments one realizes that nothing can be taken for granted; that everything has the hallmark of free gift and of grace; that one must give thanks for everything — and even that one must give thanks for being able to give thanks.

We have just said that we should not take it for granted that other people *are*. When our higher consciousness is asleep — as it mostly is — we do take their existence for granted. During the rare moments when we are fully awake we get a glimpse of the truth.

Human relationships that matter are of two kinds. One kind arises from an encounter: someone has entered into our life, from somewhere. It is always from somewhere — from somewhere unknown. For however much we know about the reasons and the immediate circumstances which lead to the meeting, how much do we *really* know of the roots of existence even of those whom we know best?

We have met, and out of this meeting something has developed which we call fellowship, friendship, or love, as the case may be. This is endowed with profound significance; for when it has come about, we feel it could not have been otherwise. Yet it might well have been otherwise; it might never have happened at all.

The other kind of relationship is rooted in life itself. The child springs from the life of the parents, and for this reason it is intimately connected with them and with its brothers and sisters. Their solidarity is not brought about by extraneous circumstances but by innate necessity — or so, at least, it would appear. But is it really so?

Father, mother, and child; brother and sister — each one of them is an individual, a person, and therefore free. For this reason, not even blood relationship should be taken for granted. Its true significance can be realized only in the light of this individual freedom.

Once this is understood, blood relationships become as reassuring, and at the same time as wonderful and *given*, as relationships that spring from encounters. It follows that we must give thanks also for the *givenness* of our parents, of our brothers and sisters, and of our children.

Thanksgiving is due for the myriad events of life

The same holds good for everything that happens in life. Natural science, the administrators, planners, and all those other experts concerned with directing human affairs have taught us to judge everything from the point of view of ascertainable laws. We are therefore conditioned to believe that things happen either because it is in their very nature that they should happen or in accordance with conditions laid down for them by man. In this way life is systematically robbed of its mystery and as a result we are disenchanted.

Many people feel that it is wrong to think in these terms, not only because it deprives life of so much of its beauty but also because it is fundamentally untrue. There are indeed moments — rare moments of illumination — when the most ordinary objects and commonplace events appear to us suddenly quite different. All at once they shed the shackles of arid matter-of-factness and become free; once free, they step out of the prison of contingent existence to enter the realm of mystery. In such moments we realize that they form part of that hidden pattern of which natural laws and human planning are but the visible projection.

We may express this in a different way: all cosmic processes, all phenomena and events to which our sensory perception and intellect give us access, occur within a system of laws — the very same laws to which perception and intellect are themselves subjected. But the system, as such, is but an instrument in the hand of God's creative freedom; at the same time it is an expression and proof of the consistency with which this freedom works.

Thus everything that happens, and everything which is, has the character of a gift of grace — and must be included in our thanksgiving.

Thanksgiving is due for God's Providence

When discussing petition in prayer, we found that fundamentally our demands are not concerned with the necessities of life or with help in distress, but with everything that comes to us from the divine superabundance through which we have our being. Our existence is encompassed by a double arc, one part of which ascends from us to God and the other — the more important — descends from God to us. Prayer is the continuous call by man for the descending arc, and thanksgiving is the completion of the arc from man to God.

Man says to God: "I thank Thee, O Lord, that I have my being in and through Thee; I thank Thee that I see with Thy light, act through Thy power, and am sanctified by Thy love."

Our relations to our fellows, to all things, and to all events obtain their true significance from our relationship to God. People, things, and events come to us as parts and aspects of the same world to which we also belong, but they are also messengers and manifestations of the loving governance of God.

That divine governance may prevail and the will of God be done is the real prayer of the Christian. His thanks consist in accepting life, with ever growing awareness, as God's gift.

Thanksgiving is due for God's existence

There is an attitude of mind which confers on thanksgiving a truly exalted, almost divine character: when man thanks and praises God for His glory and for His very being. But how is this possible? Have we not just said that we can give thanks only for what we receive neither by necessity nor by right? What can be more necessary in this sense than the existence of God, of whom it is said that He is by His very existence "worthy . . . to receive glory, and honor, and power: because Thou hast created all things; and for Thy will they were and have been created."[41]

Yet even God's existence cannot be taken for granted, although not in the sense in which the existence of the world cannot be taken for granted. The world *is* because it has pleased God to create it. God *is* because He is the mystery in itself, the living substantial miracle.

In its original, proper sense, *mystery* does not signify something unexplained which requires, or indeed is capable of, explanation; it signifies that which pertains to the nature of the Deity. *Miracle* is not in the first place a phenomenon or occurrence which goes beyond the possibilities of known laws; it is a sign from God — a state of transfiguration in which the most ordinary object and commonplace event suddenly shines in the light of God.

Whoever is in the proximity of God experiences His mystery and His all-compelling might and thus knows that he is in the

[41]Rev. 4:11.

presence of the One who alone is real, substantial, and necessary, the One who calls forth the holy awe in man. From this awe springs thanksgiving.

When we love someone truly — that is, if we feel not merely respect, sympathy, or desire, but are linked to him or her by that bond of inmost *belonging* — we are filled with a sense of constant wonderment, almost awe toward the beloved person. It may reach a degree of intensity which makes us want to explain it: "I thank you for being as you are; I thank you for *being*." Such things cannot be rationally explained, but the heart understands them. With man this mystery can be no more than an intimation; with God it finds its full consummation.

Thanksgiving is due constantly

It is therefore of the utmost importance that we should learn to give thanks. We must do away with the indifference which takes all things for granted, for nothing is to be taken for granted — everything is a gift. Not until man has understood this will he truly be free.

In the morning, when we are rested from the night and are filled with a pure and exhilarating feeling of life, we should say to God: "I thank Thee that I am permitted to live; I thank Thee that I breathe and that I am; and I thank Thee for all I have and for all that is around me." After meals we should say: "What I have partaken of is Thy gift; I thank Thee." In the evening we should say: "That I was permitted to live today; to work, to rejoice; that I met this person; that I became aware of that other person's loyalty — all that Thou hast given me; for all that I thank Thee."

We should give thanks for our faith, for the mystery of our rebirth in Christ, for all the hidden and holy bonds between the Creator and ourselves. We should endeavor to extend our thanks to include also all that which is difficult, hard, or incomprehensible in our lives: it is all part of grace. That it should be so is the one aspect of the message of Providence which is for us the most difficult to understand, and demands of us the greatest fortitude — but it is also the one which holds the greatest promise.

To live in harmony with Providence means to live in obedience to the will of God — also against one's own desires. This submission finds its purest expression in the gratitude which gladly accepts hardship and what appears to be injury from the hands of God. This is not easy and we should not deceive ourselves. We should never go beyond what our sense of truthfulness will permit. But we are capable of greater things than we think at first. Sustained by faith, thanksgiving can extend to tribulations and, in the measure in which it succeeds, it will transform them.

Summary of the basic acts of prayer

Now let us look back. We have said that in the condition of recollectedness we become aware of the reality of God. We have tried to show how this reality reveals its diverse facets and calls forth the different forms of prayer.

First we spoke of the holiness of God. This calls forth in us awareness of our own unworthiness, acknowledgment of our guilt, repentance, and new resolve. It also calls forth the awareness that God is the Savior and awakens the desire for Him and the longing for union with Him.

We then spoke of the majesty of God. We respond to it by adoration — the act of homage signifying our complete yet voluntary surrender to God's almighty power. As we rejoice over the glory of God, adoration becomes praise.

Finally we spoke of the bountifulness of God's ever giving love. To His love we appeal in prayer for our many needs; yet ultimately all our needs may be summed up in the one all-embracing need: to live in the grace of God. By acknowledging as God's gift our entire existence, we give thanks.

Thus various facets of God's being reveal themselves. We respond with various facets of our own being, and in so doing become ourselves, for only before God and in the measure in which we receive the truth from Him and respond to it, do we become aware of our humanity.

In the foregoing we discussed those forms of prayer which stand out most clearly; but there are many other forms. God is inexhaustible, and man is — to paraphrase an expression by Anselm of Canterbury — the inexhaustible in the sight of God. Man is (and today even natural science concedes this) not merely a living being among other living beings, but the very principle of life. Hence he is able to respond to God, and this response is, of its very nature, prayer.

Thus there is prayer which responds to the remoteness of God — to His hiddenness and to His unknownness. Conversely, there is prayer which responds to His nearness, His openness, and His accessibility. There is prayer which springs from the direct comprehension of the truth — prayer which is, as it were, a spontaneous confession of faith.

But there is also prayer which is a confession of ignorance, an admission of failure before the mystery. There is the prayer of plenitude, when God's presence is fully experienced; but there is also the prayer of privation when it appears that God has forsaken us, leaving a great void which nothing can fill.

There are times when everything seems intelligible and familiar, and there are times when nothing seems to make sense or to be worthwhile, when there is no hope and no one to turn to — times when we must persevere in silence. All these different times demand their own forms of prayer.

Yet all forms of prayer belong together. If we were merely conscious of our unworthiness without the reassuring thought that, in spite of it, we belong to God, we could not pray. On the other hand, when we yearn for God we become acutely aware of our failings and imperfections. If we were to make light of them, our yearning would lack humility. Again, if we were unable to apprehend the glory of God and to rejoice over it, the feeling of His power would overawe us. Then again, when praising God we might easily be led into unseemly flattery unless restrained by the awe which His holiness inspires in us.

Petition and thanksgiving are complementary: they are our way of acknowledging the great mystery of divine love to which we owe our existence. Thus a short reflection teaches us that adoration and repentance, yearning and praise, thanksgiving and communion, petition and reverence, are all interconnected. They are but different aspects of the living relationship of man to God, made possible because God reveals Himself to man and calls him.

3

The Most Holy Trinity and Prayer

The mystery of the triune God

The manner in which we speak to different people varies greatly. Our approach to a child is not the same as to an adult; to an intelligent person we speak in one way, to a simple-minded in another. Our way of speaking to a person also varies according to the esteem in which we hold him.

Everyone has a mental make-up and certain traits which are peculiarly his own and constitute what we call his *individuality*. Only when we establish contact with this individuality can we truly hold converse with a person.

But there is more to it than this. A variation of approach is also necessary in relation to animals. As every animal lover knows, animals possess different and greatly varying dispositions and he will therefore try to adapt his approach accordingly.

With human beings, however, it is not only a question of disposition, or even of individuality. The human being is *person*.

Each human is a person

Although we all know what we mean by *person*, it is difficult to put exactly into words. We may think of it as the inmost core and coordinating center of man's individuality. We may think of it as the point of origin from which man goes forth into the world and to which he returns; the fulcrum of consciousness in which he takes his stand as a responsible being — the inner face of his *selfhood*. In short, *person* is what a man means when he says "I."

When we ask somebody, "What kind of a person are you?" he will answer by describing his work or profession, his conditions of life, his origin, his character. But if we ask him, "Who are you?" he will say, "I am X," giving his name, which stands for the uniqueness of his being. The entity which describes itself with the personal pronoun *I* is the person. It is ever present but is not always in the foreground. Sometimes it does not appear at all, sometimes only imperfectly, as, for example, when actions are purely mechanical or instinctive.

Although his status of *person* is the birthright of man, to maintain it is an exacting task which demands his constant attention. We are only too ready to abandon it (and to seek refuge in a *depersonalized* state which frees us from responsibility) when faced by a crisis or a moral issue which demands a clear and immediate decision.

The *person* also comes into its own when we enter into a close relationship with another. Indeed, a close relationship (that is, a relationship which gives rise to a mutual feeling of esteem and obligation) can come about only when people see each other's inner face through the veils of their outer *personality*.

In God, too, there is person, but in a manner quite different from man. Man is but himself — one and alone. It is otherwise with the *personalness* of God.

God is three Divine Persons

Reading the Gospels carefully we are struck by the distinctive way in which the Divine declares itself in and around Christ, and also by the way in which Christ addresses God and keeps company with Him. For Christ there is but one God — the Living, the Holy, the Creator and Lord of the Universe. This *one* God, however, reveals Himself with different faces. Thus Christ repeatedly speaks of the *Father* with whom He is in closest communion, whom He obeys also in the moment of most intense spiritual anguish — as is shown by the words spoken in the Garden of Gethsemane: "Not as I will, but as Thou wilt."[42] Yet Christ's relationship to the Father is altogether different from that of any one of us. He is His Son in a manner impossible for man. Never did Christ, when speaking to man, include Himself when He said "Our Father"; never did He include Himself with mankind in turning together with them to the Father; never did He say the Lord's Prayer together with those to whom He taught it. When He said that men should all become "children of God," He meant by this relationship something substantially different from the Father-Son relationship expressed by the words: "All things are delivered to me by my Father; and no one knoweth who the Son is, but the Father; and who the Father is, but the Son, and to whom the Son will reveal Him."[43] Christ obeys the Father but not in the manner in which the creature obeys the Creator; Christ's obeying is on equal footing with God's commanding — it is equally divine. Before the face of the Father rises the divine face of the Son.

A third "face," which is much more difficult to comprehend, rises when Jesus speaks to the disciples telling them that (when He

[42]Matt. 26:39.
[43]Luke 10:22.

has gone away) "I will ask the Father, and He shall give you another Paraclete, that He may abide with you for ever. The Spirit of truth, whom the world cannot receive, because it seeth Him not, nor knoweth Him: but you shall know Him; because He shall abide with you, and shall be in you. I will not leave you orphans, I will come to you. . . . But the Paraclete, the Holy Spirit, whom the Father will send in my name, He will teach you all things, and He will bring all things to your mind, whatsoever I shall have said to you."[44] It is the Holy Spirit who came to the apostles at Pentecost and who has taken on the heritage of Christ and the government of the Church.

The Gospels reveal the Trinity to us

A great mystery is here revealed. God whose essence and being surpasses everything human is also *person* in a different and quite stupendous way. Man is only one person — the one which he expresses by the word *I*. In God, however, there are three who speak thus. Triple is the face of His being, triple the way in which His life is master of itself.

When man wishes to say "thou" he must go outside himself. God, however, finds the "thou" within His own being. Man depends on others for company: on his parents, brothers or sisters, husband or wife, children, friends, colleagues, or working companions. God, however, the One and Only, has this company within Himself. This is the ultimate meaning of the divine attributes *living* and *bountiful*.

The New Testament gives two interpretations of the holy mystery, of three persons united in one God. Of the first, mention

[44]John 14:16-18, 26.

has been made. It is akin to the relationship between the first and second generation — in other words, between parents and children. The mystery of generation is enacted in God. From all eternity God is *Father* (in this concept earthly paternity and maternity are fused in perfect unity) and He is also *Son* (the concept here includes son and daughter, symbolizing the heirs of life). As Father, God gives to the Son the fullness of His own life and being. But the Son does not leave the Father, does not become God, as it were, in His own right, but remains in the living unity, turns lovingly toward the Father, "is in the bosom of the Father."[45]

That the whole freedom of Sonship may be realized and that the Son's independence may not destroy the divine unity is made possible by another holy force which is also substantial and which is named the *Holy Spirit*. He is the very love that passes between the Father and the Son.

There is another interpretation. It is given at the beginning of the Gospel according to St. John. According to it, God is aware of Himself; He knows the infinity of His own being. God uttered Himself in the created word. Thus God is the Speaker and that which is spoken. That which is spoken, however — the *Word* or *Logos* — is as mighty as the speaker, living and consubstantial. The Word is not a message to be heard by someone else; it is both message and the ear that hears it; it is the speaker being heard by Himself. The Word is the speaker become manifest. This is the meaning of the text "The Word was with God and the Word was God."[46]

The one whom we have called the speaker is the Father; that which He spoke — the Word — is the Son. It is the Holy Spirit in whom dwells this mystery of the unity in Trinity.

[45]John 1:18.
[46]John 1:1.

The Gospel has revealed this divine mystery to us, and the redemption has made it possible for us to share in it. The eternally begotten Son — the *Logos* — has come to dwell among us, has become flesh and shared our existence.

In so doing He has gathered us up into His own existence. He has proclaimed to us the mystery of the renewal: man who has his first natural life — who is born of the flesh — has been assumed into the divine womb, from there to be reborn into the new life of the children of God. He has been chosen to share the place which Christ has with God — to become Christ's brother and sister.

So he should go with Christ to the Father as His son or daughter, not by substance, but through grace, and this should come about by the power of the Holy Spirit who is his friend and comforter.

We pray not to a vague concept of deity, but to the real and responsible God who has revealed Himself to us and who has told us His name. Our prayer must go out to Him as He has declared Himself to us — as the *triune* God. Thus Christian prayer is communion with the Trinity.

Prayer to the Son

In attempting to discuss prayer to the Son, it would seem to be appropriate to begin with the prayer to the Father, but it would be wrong, for the Father is a mystery. He is not merely the all-mighty, all-caring one, as described by most religions. In Himself He is the unknown God; He becomes known only in His Son. The Son, Christ, opens the door to the mystery of the living three-in-one God. Christ is, as He Himself said, "the door."[47] But "no man hath

---

[47]John 10:9.

seen God at any time: the only begotten Son who is in the bosom of the Father, He hath declared Him."[48]

Spiritual life begins with prayer to the Son

The correct procedure of Christian prayer must begin by entering into the right relationship with Christ. He has become our brother. He is the firstborn; we are His brethren, says St. Paul.[49] He is the Master; we are the disciples. "One is your master; and all you are brethren."[50] He is the one who leads us, who knows the way, who is the example. We are the ones who must follow Him. "I am the way, and the truth, and the life. No man cometh unto the Father, but by me."[51] He is the one who reveals; He is the living manifestation of the Father. We behold His face, and "he that seeth me seeth the Father also."[52]

Praying to Christ means entering into this relationship, understanding it, enacting it. Praying to Christ, therefore, is not in the first place adoring Him or asking for His help. Of course it includes also this — implicitly, for Christ is God whom we adore and to whom we pray for help. But the real prayer to Christ consists in dwelling in the relationship which He has established. In this prayer the worshipper beseeches Christ to vouchsafe that he may understand Him; he beholds the Lord, ponders over His life and His words, tries to enter into His truth. He seeks instruction and enlightenment in Christ's holy teaching; he asks what he should do in order to follow Him and takes his life into the radiance of

[48]John 1:18.
[49]Rom. 8:29.
[50]Matt. 23:8.
[51]John 14:6.
[52]John 14:9.

Christ's words and actions. He asks Christ for His love; he tries to grasp the meaning of that love which is so different from earthly love and he endeavors to let it prevail in his own life.

He strives to be worthy of the redemption and asks Christ to intercede for him with the Father. He prays that he may be included in the new covenant and appeals to the mystery of renewal so that it may realize itself in him.

In praying to Christ we seek the countenance of the Son who became man for us, and do so with full confidence, knowing that Christ is not merely a figure of bygone history (which has left certain proofs in the records of his ministry). We know that Christ lives; we know that Christ who once was, still is, and will be for evermore. He is, and will be, not far away — not departed into the inaccessible light of His glory — but close by, abiding with every one of us, so that every one may say, "The Lord cares for me; His face is turned toward me; He effects my salvation; He loves me."

By earnestly endeavoring to follow Christ, we attune our will to His, for it is Christ's will to be a reality and force in man. What man endeavors to work with his own limited strength on earth, Christ works in heaven, and to Christ all power is given.

Christ dwells within us

St. Paul repeatedly speaks of the mystery that Christ is not merely above us and with us, but *in* us. When He rose from the dead He became once more man in the fullest sense of the word, but it was a changed humanity to which He rose. He was transfigured and spiritualized, freed of the limitations of space and time, freed of the restriction of matter, and able therefore to enter into man without doing violence to man's dignity.

Thus the intimate, holy mystery was made possible in which Christ is in the believer and the believer in Him. It constitutes the ultimate significance of our relationship to the eternal Son of God. In the encounter with Christ, the polarity of separateness merges into a mysterious oneness.

To believe means to be convinced of this union — to be aware of it. To live a Christian life means to live in the spirit of the union; to pray to Christ means to give expression to one's awareness of it. The awareness is prepared in Baptism, founded in faith, and finally confirmed in the Eucharist, in which Christ becomes the food of life. Thus by partaking of the bread which is His body and of the wine which is His blood, we consummate that relationship which is expressed in the words: "He that eateth my flesh, and drinketh my blood, abideth in me, and I in him."[53] Prayer to Christ dwells on this mystery.

Prayer to the Father

It is only through Christ that we come to the Father. When speaking of God the Father, we ought to add that we mean Him whom Christ means when He says "My Father." Thus we would signify that we were not thinking of a vague concept of deity whose power one may suspect behind the government of the world, but that holy countenance which revealed itself for the first time in the words of Christ.

We must go with Christ to the Father

When we "go to the Father,"[54] we must go together with Christ, along His path and in His spirit. There can be no other way to the Father than the one on which the Son came to us.

[53]John 6:57.
[54]John 14:13, 28.

So that we may be able to follow Christ, we must never cease to dwell on His life and teaching; otherwise our prayer to God will inevitably assume the character of a vague cosmic worship. Only through Christ can we reach the real Father in heaven.

The Lord's Prayer leads us to the Father

Christ has laid down for us how we should pray to the Father. When His disciples came to Him and said, "Lord, teach us to pray, as John also taught his disciples," He answered, "When ye pray, say" — and He said the Lord's Prayer.[55]

No words have been uttered more often by human lips than those of the Lord's Prayer. Unfortunately it has lost much of its true significance and become, with many who pray, no more than a convenient way of giving expression to a general, unfocused mood of piety.

When we speak the words "Our Father," we often have no more than a nebulous notion of some high authority; when we say "hallowed be Thy name," we experience a general sort of reverence; when we speak of "the kingdom," we imagine something vaguely akin to a general state of good-will among men.

Rightly understood, and spoken in the spirit in which Christ taught them, the words of the Lord's Prayer have profound and eternal significance. Their key lies in the body of teaching which is known as the Sermon on the Mount. They are illumined by the parables in which Christ explains the relationship between God and man (such as, for example, by the parable of the Prodigal Son); thus, if rightly understood in this wider context, they become a living path leading us to the Father.

---

[55]Luke 11:1.

Because the Lord's Prayer is so full of meaning and truth, and yet so simple, it frequently suffers the fate of being said thoughtlessly, without true reverence and inner intent. It happens so much that we ought to remind ourselves of our responsibility as Christians to preserve and treasure Christ's holy heritage. We should say the Lord's Prayer in a recollected mood, thoughtfully, and putting our heart into its words. Only then will it open the doors to the kingdom of the Father which the Son's love has prepared for us.

Prayer to the Holy Spirit

When Christ for the last time, shortly before His death, assembled His disciples, He spoke to them thus: "But the Paraclete, the Holy Spirit, whom the Father will send in my name, He will teach you all things, and bring all things to your mind, whatsoever I shall have said to you."[56]

The Holy Spirit helps us to know Christ

It is impossible to understand and accept Christ in the manner in which we understand and accept other historical figures. In Him the Son of God has become man and dwells among us. This is a mystery so profound that it surpasses the power of our intellect; it is also a judgment on the world which forces us to change our entire mode of thinking and reassess all our values.

Unaided, we cannot understand Christ. The faculty of understanding can be awakened only by the One who is Christ's equal — the Holy Spirit through whose power the Son of God became man. The Holy Spirit opens the heart and the mind, and our

[56]John 14:26.

prayer to Him is the prayer by which we ask that we may understand Christ.

As a historical figure Christ is easily blurred by similarity with other historical figures, and also by the fact that man has an instinctive aversion to anything which goes beyond the purely human. The Holy Spirit must grant us the gift of discrimination. The figure of Christ, as well as His message, is surrounded by misunderstandings, distortions, and hostility.

The Holy Spirit must give assurance to our hearts and minds so that we may find the way to Him. Christ is the truth. The Holy Spirit must give us this understanding of Christ, which in the words of St. Paul "surpasses everything,"[57] and must awaken our love for Him.

The Holy Spirit teaches us to understand Christ, and in Christ, God and ourselves. It is the kind of understanding which comes from the heart, not from the intellect. It is true comprehension; more than that, it is illumination.

The Holy Spirit gives the answers to those questions which the mind cannot answer because the mind invariably couples the word *why* with the word *I*. "Why must *I* endure this suffering? Why am *I* denied what others have? Why must *I* be the way I am, live the way I do?" These are some of the most essential and decisive questions in the life of the individual, and to those questions men and books remain silent. The true answer comes only when our heart is free from revolt and bitterness; when our will has come to terms with life *as it is for us*, recognizing in it the working of the will of God.

The intellect may acquiesce readily enough, but this is not sufficient. Instruction must go deeper; acceptance must come from

[57]Eph. 3:19.

our inmost heart. Only then will we find the answer to the *why*, and with it, peace, for truth alone brings peace. This is the work of the Holy Spirit.

The Holy Spirit strengthens faith, hope, and love

The Church has in its sacred books some wonderful prayers to the Holy Spirit which convey much more than any words of explanation. The beautiful sequence *Veni, Sancte Spiritus* — so full of unutterable peace — from the Mass of Pentecost springs to mind; or the hymn from the Vespers of the same feast (*Veni, Creator Spiritus*) with its expression of boundless confidence.

It is much more difficult to speak of the Holy Spirit than of the Son or the Father. He eludes us; it is as though He said, "Not I but the Son." He is the humble, the selfless One who works in secret, who has no other wish than to give to us what is of Christ. Songs such as those just mentioned, which rise from the heart, get nearer to Him than anything which comes from the mind.

Finally, the hope of the Christian is linked to the Holy Spirit. Our life is shrouded in insufficiency and darkness. Faith teaches us that there is a mysterious process of *becoming* in us: the becoming of the new man, fashioned in the image of Christ, and the becoming of the new heaven and the new earth of which the secret Revelation speaks.

But this becoming is hidden — and everything we perceive within ourselves and around us seems to belie it. Therefore we stand in need of hope, which springs from the Holy Spirit; for it is He who effects this becoming. He is the recreator of creation; He fashions the future which is to become eternity. He alone can assure us of this future.

Our own being is hidden from us. The Scriptures tell man what he is and he must believe it. He must not only believe in God, but must accept God's message and promise about his own Christian destiny. This is not always easy and we must pray to the Holy Spirit for that inmost assurance which we call faith and hope, and which is sustained by love.

4

Oral Prayer

The words of prayer

To pray is to communicate with God; the medium of communication is the spoken word, and although we can convey feeling, desire, and intent also by facial expression and gesture, it is only by words that we can give them clarity of meaning and of form. By the word also we declare and bind ourselves. Thus in oral prayer as in any other form of speech, it matters what kind of words we use and how we use them. Right intent is in itself not enough.

It is true that clumsy and awkward words that spring from a sincere heart are preferable to the most flowery ones which are devoid of inner substance. God looks into the hearts of men and will not reject those of pure heart who find it difficult to express themselves clearly or well.

It does not follow, however, that it is unimportant what we say and how we say it. Generally speaking, right intent will produce the right words; conversely, faulty words, and more especially babbling and sentimental ones, reveal a state of mind which is itself at fault.

The words we speak will themselves affect our state of mind. Human speech does not originate with the individual as an autogenous means of self-expression; man finds the world of words — the language — ready-made for him. He is born into the language, grows up with it, and is influenced by it to an even greater extent than by his surroundings.

Language penetrates down to the roots of his mental and emotional life. He thinks in it, feels in it; it is the vehicle of intercourse with his fellows and the means by which he learns the significance and use of all objects.

The language of prayer is no exception to the rule. Only to a limited extent can the individual make up his own wording; the greater part of it he finds ready-made. It follows that the words used in prayer have a formative influence on the whole of our spiritual life; we should therefore pay due attention to them.

Spontaneous prayers

The most vital prayer is the one which springs unprompted from the heart; it has no difficulty in finding its own appropriate language. Indeed, we may say that the spontaneous expression of repentance or yearning, adoration or joy, supplication or thanksgiving, is the prime language of prayer.

Learning to speak (that is, acquiring the faculty of putting one's thoughts and feelings into words and conveying them to others) is a vital part of our growing-up process. It should be the aim of education to develop in the individual the ability not merely to use the language correctly but also in accordance with his own way of experiencing and seeing the world — in other words, to use it in an individual manner.

This also applies to the language of prayer. We do not pray merely to communicate our needs to God — He knows our hearts better than we do. Prayer is an intimate form of speaking which should bear the mark of our personality. In prayer we live before God, offer up to Him what is ours to offer, and receive from Him what it pleases Him to give to us. Therefore the language of our prayer should be truly our own.

There are times when spontaneous formulation of our prayer is easy. When we feel God's presence, or when we are in distress and put ourselves into God's merciful hand, the right words come of themselves.

Often, however, the heart is empty and the mind has little to say; in this state of poverty speech does not come easily. But we must not give up; we must accept this insufficiency, for it has its own purpose and its own significance. We must find words of prayer which are true to it, words of great simplicity — plain affirmations of faith, hope, and acceptance. Such words are not less valuable than those which flow in easy abundance, and they are the right ones for the occasion precisely because they are not contrived or artificial.

If words do not come easily we should not immediately resort to established texts; we should subject ourselves to the discipline of inner poverty. We may learn lessons from it which no sacred books can teach us.

Even if the language of our prayer consisted in nothing more than the words "I believe in Thee" or "I bow before Thee" or "I will obey Thee and do all that is in my power" or "I commend myself to Thy holy care," the prayer would be as precious before God as the most inspired flow of words in a moment of profound emotion. However, we should not go to extremes of resignation. If we cannot find the right words within, we must not hesitate to go to external sources.

The Art of Praying

The established texts of prayer

We speak of the "communion of saints" without knowing too well what is meant by it. It does not mean the communion between the saints or the communion between ordinary people like ourselves and those great ones whom we call saints. It means, above all, the company of those united by a common faith in the Gospel, the Eucharist, and all things pertaining to divine life. If, therefore, there exist appropriate and good words of prayer which have sprung from the heart of some inspired person, it is only right and proper that others should make use of them. This establishes a union in holiness.

There are other reasons why we not only may but should make use of established texts: we may learn from them. It has already been shown that speech is more than a means of individual self-expression; it is the means by which the individual moves in that vast world of symbolism which we call language.

In this world he finds much more than the individual words which have developed in the course of time; he finds combinations of words, phrases, predications, periods, and patterns of thought which others have created; he must enter into them and submit himself to their formative power.

The same again applies to the language of prayer. The texts established by pious people are imbued with their experiences and with their struggles; in using these texts we make them part of our own schooling. They not only teach us how to express our own thoughts, but can awaken in us thoughts and feelings which may have been dormant. The prayers of saints are veritable journeys of discovery in the land of the spirit, paths that lead to God — intimations of a new life. A good prayer can be to our spirit what bread is to the hungry, medicine to the sick, or flowers to those weighed down by the monotony of everyday life.

Prayers given by God Himself

There are prayers which come to us directly from God, which form part of Revelation: the Psalms, for instance. They tell us of God and how to reach Him — not in the form of instruction but directly. They take us by the hand and lead us. The Psalms are not only beautiful in themselves but are necessary to us. They originated in God-inspired hearts; they were implanted in them by God, to rise up to Him as an offering of all mankind.

The same is true of the great prayer texts in the Gospels (such as the *Magnificat*,[58] the *Benedictus*,[59] and Simeon's thanksgiving[60]). And there is one text which is of absolute validity and is necessary to us all — the Lord's Prayer. No one should say that his spiritual life is so highly developed that he has no more need of the Lord's Prayer; this would be delusion or arrogance. The Lord's Prayer must forever be our introduction to prayer: it was the Lord Himself who taught it to His disciples when they said to Him, "Teach us to pray."[61]

Yet another, more hidden, significance attaches to the prayers just mentioned: they are part of the new creation. The new man lives in them. They are mysteries, linked to the rites out of which spring the *things to come*, namely, the sacraments. When we say these prayers we help to build the new earth and the new heaven.

Not quite of the same eminence, but nevertheless connected with them, are the prayers of the Church as contained in the Liturgy. Not all liturgical prayers are equally valuable, but some of them offer wonderful opportunities for communion with God

---

[58]Luke 1:46-55.
[59]Luke 1:68-79.
[60]Luke 2:29-32.
[61]Luke 11:1.

(such as, for example, the *Gloria* of the Mass or the "Come, Holy Spirit" of the feast of Pentecost, and also some of the hymns and prayers of the Divine Office). Their texts mostly originate in the early Church; they have grandeur and give expression to a most lofty concept of God. We cannot do better than to use them also for our own personal devotions.

The importance of choosing holy prayers

It is important to choose the right kind of prayer. We are not speaking now of the revealed prayers which form part of the divine canon of prayer and are therefore binding for all, although it is left to the individual to decide which of these prayers are suited for various occasions. We are speaking now of prayers as found in certain current prayer books, and here we should not mince words. Many of these prayers are simply superfluous; others affect our spirits as bad food affects our body.

Prayer, as we have said, must above all be truthful; prayer, therefore, which is given to exaggeration is not truthful.[62] Untruthful also are prayers which are mawkish and sentimental, which presume feelings which a mentally healthy person cannot entertain. The same applies to prayers in which man abases himself before God and revels in the idea of his own sinfulness. Such prayers have unwholesome roots and must therefore be rejected.

It may appear strange to speak of a sense of honor in the context of prayer. The sense of honor is, as we know, a sentiment of problematic value, and many of its forms have no place at all in

---

[62] In the writings of the saints we often come across strong passages expressing self-contempt and self-abasement. These passages must be understood in their proper context and as expressions of the personality of the saint. They cannot be held as applying to all conditions of life, nor must they be interpreted as forming part of the basic attitude and mood of Christian life.

the realm of spiritual life. But there is a sense of honor which does enter into the relationship between man and God, not only for man's sake but also for God's sake. People speak of their honor and lay great store by it; they should remember above all that honor can be upheld only by means which are themselves honorable. In the sight of God, only the kind of prayer which springs from clean and honorable motives has real value.

Forms of repetitive prayer

In the next chapter we shall discuss contemplative prayer; here we want to deal with forms of prayer which occupy a halfway position between oral and contemplative prayer and which play an important part in Christian devotion.

In oral prayer we give expression to our feelings and needs before God. To this form of prayer apply the words in the Sermon on the Mount: "But when you are praying, speak not much words, as the heathens. For they think that in their much speaking they may be heard."[63] When we speak to God, we should do so simply, trustingly, and with reverence, and not say more than is inwardly justified. Of course, we may repeat ourselves just as we may repeat ourselves when speaking to people. There is nothing wrong with repetition as such, since it is frequently difficult to express our feelings in a single brief statement. When Christ warned His disciples against the "much words" of the heathens, He meant not so much the actual repeating of words and phrases, but the motive behind such practice — the desire to impress by the sheer number and weight of words.

[63]Matt. 6:7.

It may happen that man wishes not only to say something specific to God but desires to dwell awhile in prayer — as it were, to move quietly in it. This may be compared to going for a walk without a set destination; one takes one's time and stops on the way to rest or to look at anything which may be worthy of note.

Since discourse with God — as with a friend — in which we pour out our heart to Him and hear His answers, is an unattainable goal for man, repetitive prayer meets a profound need of the Christian. It was adopted very early by the Church and consists in the reiteration of certain pure and meaningful words or phrases within a progression of consecutive thoughts. The repetitive part of the prayer — the responses — create a series of "resting places" in which the spirit can stop awhile each time before being carried forward again by the main theme.

The Litany

A very ancient form of repetitive prayer is the Litany. It consists of a sequence of invocations to God (spoken or chanted by the officiant) and of responses (by the congregation) in the form of short sentences such as "Have mercy on us" or "Lord, hear our prayer" repeated at intervals throughout.

These short responses give resonance to the invocation, while they themselves continually gain new significance by the changing contents of the invocations. A single invocation would be over too quickly; mere repetition would be monotonous. This form of prayer, however, allows for progressive change while retaining the peace and stability of contemplation.

The full beauty of the Litany emerges only when it is said correctly. The invocations must be spoken very clearly and short pauses must be made between them and the responses, thus allowing the meaning of each invocation to linger for awhile. In this manner all automatism is avoided and the theme unfolds as an organic whole.

The Angelus

Another example of this form of prayer is the *Angelus*. It recalls three times a day — at sunrise, noon, and sunset — the event with which our redemption began: the message of the angel to Mary. This prayer is a remembrance and therefore demands that we should dwell on it in a mood of contemplation. It is full of meaning and yet so simple that it can be said wherever we happen to be — at home, in the street, at the office, when traveling, and so forth. Three short sentences, each followed by a Hail Mary, recall the event and enable us to dwell on the invocation:

> *The Angel of the Lord declared unto Mary:*
> *And she conceived of the Holy Spirit.*
>
> *Behold the handmaid of the Lord:*
> *Be it done unto me according to thy word.*
>
> *And the Word was made Flesh,*
> *And dwelt among us.*

The *Angelus* has been largely lost to modern city-dwellers who are hardly able to notice the phases of the sun or hear the church bells. Nevertheless, it should be possible for us to remind ourselves, at least at noon and in the evening, that many hearts in many lands enact this holy remembrance, and to join in with them.

The Rosary

The Rosary is another well-known form of repetitive prayer. It combines its two main characteristics (the dwelling in repetition and the slow progression) in a very perfect manner. We cannot fully enter into it here; we would first have to point out all the difficulties with which it confronts modern man and discuss the abuses and errors which are associated with it. Furthermore, we would have to explain its inner structure as well as the proper way in which it should be recited; this would go beyond the scope of this book.

The Rosary is a prayer which is not suited for all occasions, and anyone who is inwardly not at peace, or is troubled by religious problems, can do very little with it; he would be well advised to leave it alone. To benefit from the Rosary, two conditions are essential: a living faith and the ability to compose the mind and remain quiet. To recite the Rosary in a hurry is not only wrong but absolutely pointless: it must be spoken slowly and thoughtfully. If there is no time for a whole Rosary one should do one section only; it is better to recite a part in the correct manner than the whole of it with insufficient care.

In the Rosary we dwell on the person and life of our Lord within the context of the life of His Blessed Mother. We call to mind fifteen successive events — from the Annunciation to the Coronation of the Blessed Virgin in heaven — and dwell on the significance of these events, not so much as events in themselves, but as events related to, and experienced by, the one who of all people was closest to our Lord.

In the Rosary, contemplation is borne forward by the words of the Hail Mary and of the Lord's Prayer recurring throughout as its main theme. In this perfect blending of progressing contemplation with a recurring prayer theme lies the essence of the Rosary.

To recite the Rosary rightly demands practice, but once we are fully acquainted with it, it may become for us a quiet hidden land in which we may dwell and find peace, or a chapel whose doors are ever open and into which we can take the burdens of our souls.

Texts for meditation

Finally, mention should be made of the devout custom of choosing a brief holy text to serve as a device and spiritual guide for the week or for any other period of time. Such a text, we shall discover, establishes its own rapport with the events of everyday life. Often it lies dormant, but now and again it may come to life and throw new light on a particular situation and help us to understand it and to act correctly. Conversely, it may happen that a situation arises which helps us to appreciate fully the significance of the text we have chosen. Such a holy motto can prove a constant source of spiritual comfort and inspiration.

5

Inward or Contemplative Prayer

The nature of contemplative prayer

This chapter heading does not fully describe the subject. All prayer which deserves the name must be *inward*. The term *inward* is used here to describe a form of prayer which moves, as it were, away from the spoken word and toward silence.

As to *contemplative*, this term is rather too wide and general to describe a form of prayer whose main feature (or trend) is to draw away the soul from the manifoldness of mental activity and to enable it to become single-pointed. The term *meditation* also does not fully convey this meaning. Of the two, *contemplative prayer* is probably the more accurate term — so long as we bear in mind the sense in which the word *contemplative* is used.

This form of prayer stands in a very special relationship to truth. Oral or spoken prayer — also an inadequate description — addresses itself to God for a specific purpose. Although it is rooted in the truth of faith, it does not directly concern itself with this truth. In spoken prayer we adore, beseech, or give thanks. Contemplative prayer, however, is concerned with the truth as such. It tries to apprehend the nature of God, to grasp the meaning of the kingdom of God, to gain insight into the condition of man and an understanding of one's own place in the pattern of things, to obtain a true picture of the world.

This search after truth is far more than an endeavor of the intellect; if it were merely that it would find its expression in theology or philosophy. It is an endeavor of an entirely different order, in which the whole of man is involved. With the faculty of imagination we focus on and visualize the theme or subject of our contemplation; with our intellectual-critical faculties we probe, scrutinize, compare; we try to distinguish between the essential and the incidental, between end and means, between the valid and nonvalid. Our feelings cannot remain detached in this spiritual quest. We shall experience in turn elation and dejection, kinship and loneliness, yearning and fulfillment.

When contemplative prayer is rightly practiced it will sooner or later tend to become very simple. To begin with, we usually need for it an extensive subject matter, which we can approach in many different ways and with a wide range of notions, considerations, expectations, and resolutions. Step by step, however, the subject of contemplation will become both simpler and more compelling. Our thoughts will diminish in number but gain in depth and concentration. The words will come more sparingly, and ultimately the inward prayer is resolved in silence or even in something which goes beyond the duality of speech and silence.

The proper motives for contemplative prayer

We do not seek the awareness which comes to us in contemplation for its own sake. We seek it so that it may guide our actions.

Contemplation asks not only what things are but also what they should be. It asks not only "What am I?" but also "What am I meant to become? What should I refrain from doing? What must I overcome? And what must I do?"

By contemplative prayer we seek to strengthen and to give direction to our will in order to master the confusion of life and to create the conditions for better and more fruitful action. Contemplative prayer must not induce a state of dreaminess and unreality; on the contrary, we must remain alert throughout, conscious of the relationship to God which we are trying to establish. Contemplative prayer should be a living encounter between man and God in which man strives to get nearer to God and in so doing to become purer, simpler, and more substantial.

Although contemplative prayer may also concern itself with moral questions and problems of ordinary life, this is not its proper domain. What we are striving to apprehend in contemplation are not the truths of the empirical world and of existential experience, but the truths of divine Revelation that have come to us in the word of God and the life of Christ.

There is something very special about revealed truth. It contains the most profound essence-being of the world and of man; but it expresses it as seen by God, embedded in the self-manifestation of God — God who is hidden and unknown, who declares Himself only through Christ.

This revelation is embedded in His message on the meaning of existence, which thus becomes the judgment of the All-Holy over the defection of man and at the same time a call to conversion. Revelation does not mean that a higher plane of cosmic knowledge opens itself to us, but that the holy God calls to man — who is shut in and isolated by his willfulness — asking man to turn toward Him and understand the meaning of existence through the word of God.

It is not demanded of us that we should learn hitherto unknown facts and inner connections. It is demanded of us that we should accept aspects of truth which we can receive only from the mouth of God and that we should make the truth our own through faith. To make this truth our own we must grow into it, become one with it.

Our willfulness resists this. Understanding therefore demands that we should change not only our ways but our way of seeing and of judging, our sense of what is true and what is false, of what is real and what is appearance, and, generally, our sense of value. Our spirit must work its way into the holy words; our heart must get accustomed to them. Only by doing so shall we be able to grasp the divine message.

The difference between Christian faith and Christian consciousness

We can also reach the heart of the matter by pointing to the distinction between Christian faith and Christian consciousness. Christian faith means that man accepts divine Revelation as the very basis of his life and remains rooted in it in loyalty and love. Christian consciousness means more than that.

Broadly speaking, consciousness is the experience of being aware — which includes thought and judgment — and of being aware in one's own particular manner. Consciousness can be called *Christian* if its particular manner of experiencing — of thinking and judging — causes it to consider true that which is true from the standpoint of divine Revelation, to consider possible that which is possible from the standpoint of divine Revelation, and to consider good, beautiful, noble, and satisfying, whatever deserves these attributes as seen from that standpoint.

We need only look around to see that this is not so. We do find Christian faith (frequently faith of a very courageous and pure form) but consciousness seems on the whole to be completely outside faith.

This is where contemplative prayer has a special task to fulfill. In contemplative prayer the believer tries to visualize the holy message, tries to understand what it contains, tries to penetrate into its inner core, tries to accept its pattern and to accustom himself to its order. This is how change in our way of seeing, thinking, and judging can come about: by this transformation of our willfulness without which there can be no true conversion.

Remote preparation for contemplative prayer

This book deals with practical things. We must ask ourselves about the right way to set about contemplation. Once again the first and most important step is preparation and here we must distinguish between what we might call the more distant and the more immediate preparation.

The more distant one consists in selecting and preparing the subject of contemplation. This cannot be done in a haphazard manner. We must know where to begin and we must know what kind of subjects there are for contemplation. It could be some article of faith or some thought by an enlightened person.

The most appropriate subject, however, will always be the Scriptures and, above all, the person and the life of Jesus Christ. His words "I am the way, and the truth, and the life"[64] express in the clearest possible manner what is involved in contemplation: the way from the Father to us and from us to the Father, the holy truth which reveals itself along this way, and the life which we partake of in Christ.

[64]John 14:6.

There are many books on contemplation, some of which are extremely useful for beginners. They give the key to understanding passages in the Scriptures and show us the lessons which may be drawn from them. In the long run, however, such ready-made contemplations are rather artificial and miss the essential thing. The essential thing is the divine presence as revealed to us in the Scriptures; therefore the book of contemplation proper is no other than the Bible itself.

Our preparation, then, consists in selecting an appropriate text. One might choose, for example, one of the Gospels or the Acts of the Apostles, or one of the Epistles and take a passage from any of these every day. It should not be too long, lest we lose control over it; nor should it be too short. One might choose, for example, one event in the life of Christ or a passage from His teaching. As time goes on we need less and less until we reach a point when one sentence is sufficient.

We should prepare the text, having selected it beforehand, preferably the evening before, so that it is ready in the morning. We should then decide on the main idea or point of view which is to govern the contemplation or on the particular question to which the contemplation is to supply the answer. If necessary, we should consult some commentary or exposition so as to be quite clear about the meaning of the text.

All this belongs to what we called the more distant preparation. The immediate preparation is even more important.

Immediate preparation for contemplative prayer

Everything that has been said in the first chapter of this book on general preparation for prayer applies here and it applies to an even higher degree. In spoken prayer the words themselves and the contents of the prayer help to keep the prayer alive. With purely contemplative prayer the danger that it might become dull or apathetic or that it might peter out is much greater, and we must guard against this.

Recollection

We must insist that outward attitude is of the greatest importance. It must ensure two things: tranquillity and alertness. It is up to the individual to decide whether kneeling, sitting, or walking is most conducive to this state.

The next step is to become quiet and still: still in body, quiet in one's thoughts, quiet in one's mind and heart and in one's whole being. We must concentrate on the thought that there is nothing of importance at this moment except prayer; we must do away with everything which does not strictly belong to the task at hand; we must collect our thoughts and be present. These preparations are in themselves prayer, and even if we spend a considerable time over them, the time will have been well spent.

Visualization

Having thus composed and recollected ourselves, we turn to the text and dwell on it. We can do so sentence by sentence, always pausing at the end of a sentence in order to consider it and enter into its meaning. The masters of the spiritual life advise that we should, when contemplating, make use of our imagination. For example, we should visualize an incident such as the miracle of the draught of fishes as vividly as we can. We should be present in mind as though we had just stopped on our way and were witnessing the event. This is most useful because it brings the event to life and makes it part of our inner experience. Of course, not everybody is able to do that. Many people completely lack the power of imagination and might not even be able to visualize the scene. Others lack the power to hold it, so that it quickly dissolves. They should not force themselves, but should rely more on thinking without visualization.

Thinking is also important for the person with a vivid imagination. The term *contemplate* means to reflect on and carefully work through a subject. This is what we should do with the chosen text. In this manner we should endeavor to acquaint ourselves with it and to penetrate into its deeper meaning.

However — we have mentioned this before — we should not approach this text with our intellect only, as though it were a scientific problem: our heart must take part in it. Thinking must become pondering, reflecting, entering, and contacting; thinking must go beyond thinking, for the truth which we are trying to apprehend is wisdom, which we might define as knowledge of the heart and instructedness of the whole of our being.

Contemplation transforms thought into prayer

Thus thought itself becomes prayer, and it is right that it should be so because contemplation is not a form of study but is conversation with God. If we have sufficient power of visual imagination, then we should attempt to converse with Christ as though He were actually present. If we are unable to do this, we should remind ourselves that our Lord, on whose life we are meditating, is present with us at all times, not just vaguely and remotely, but here and now. The Christ of whom the Gospels speak abides with us, and He abides with us in a very special way: it is He who indicates the meeting place to us. If the worshipper had the psychic faculty of "seeing" the situation as a whole — that is to say, himself and the circumstances at the moment of prayer — he would understand that the situation was brought about in the first place by Christ's presence. Thus it is not so that man, having decided of his own power to seek our Lord, then finds his way to Him; it is our Lord who is there first and who calls to man: "Approach and be with me." This is the precondition which makes prayer possible and enables us to offer up to God our faith and love and put before Him whatever is in our hearts.

Contemplation transforms life

This does not exhaust the meaning and purpose of contemplation. Contemplation must affect life itself. However, we must not interpret this in too narrow a sense. Some people think that unless some specific error has been clarified or some definite resolve has emerged, contemplation has not served its purpose. This is a mistaken view. To dwell for awhile in the presence of Christ in contemplation is in itself a holy and salutary event which may affect us profoundly; for whenever we apprehend some particular trait of His holy character or appreciate the significance of one of His sayings, our spirit is enriched.

At the same time we must not disregard our own personal and immediate problems. The Apostle says: "What things soever were written, were written for our learning."[65] Thus a road leads into our life from every word in the Gospels. In their light we see how things stand with us. We feel a sense of guidance and it becomes clear to us what we ought to do and what we ought to avoid or overcome. This leads — or ought to lead — to clear decisions and resolves regarding our conduct of life and our duties toward God and man. These resolves should be made before God and should become part of our life.

[65]Rom. 15:4.

From such repeated self-examination there slowly emerges a better understanding of one's own character, of one's faults, and of one's good and bad potentialities; a better insight also into life and its tasks; also a better understanding of the people with whom we are brought into daily contact. In this manner we are being instructed from within and acquire a new security which we could not gain in any other way.

It is of paramount importance — we must repeat this — for contemplation to become prayer. The worshipper must reach out to the living God, must become aware of His holy presence, must seek out His holy countenance and enter into His heart. Contemplation should become a real dialogue in which man's *I* faces its true *Thou*, which is God. This is what fundamentally matters, so much so that there would be no further need for questioning, considering, and resolve, provided that this holy encounter were brought about at the very outset.

Contemplative prayer tends toward silence

We mentioned that contemplative prayer has the tendency to become ever simpler and more silent. As we gain experience in this form of prayer we need fewer and fewer thoughts, until finally one single thought may be sufficient to find the way to truth and God. Fewer thoughts demand fewer words. St. Francis used the phrase "My God and my all" as his theme of contemplation for a whole night.

In contemplation our mode of thinking changes. From its usual restlessness it becomes a quiet beholding and a comprehending, a watching and a witnessing. Our voice changes: it becomes softer and lower. Finally, speech dies down and its place is taken by a silent regarding and longing between the soul and God. If we should reach this stage in contemplation, we should not force ourselves back into the diversity of thought. This would not only be useless; it would be harmful. When simplicity contains the essence, there is no need for diversity; when silence is eloquent, it is greater than words.

There are people to whom a profusion of thought and words are alien. With them, the state of quietude, which others take considerable time to establish, is very quickly reached. They require only very few words; anything beyond it would merely confuse them. They may not even need any words or thoughts in order to establish the state of mind in which they experience the presence of God. If that is so, they need not search any farther. They should, however, not take this for granted. It may happen that on another occasion they need a proper subject for contemplation and must have recourse to a proper text.

We cannot do more here than give a general description of the character and practice of contemplative prayer. It must take different forms with different people. Thus what we have said should not be regarded as a general rule but merely as a survey which may give some guidance in individual cases.

Some people find contemplation very much easier than others. Some people are by nature quieter and more introspective than others who are highly strung and permanently keyed up for action. Again, the form of contemplation must vary with individual disposition. The slow, plodding, and methodical person will set about it in a different way from someone who is quick and impressionable, the imaginative person in a different way from the abstract thinker.

There are no general rules. What matters is that we should seek the truth and that through truth we should strive after God. Also, contemplation changes in character with time and circumstances. It comes more easily when life is serene and reasonably successful than when we are harassed and inwardly distraught. At times it is a profound joy. Sometimes it entails considerable effort. When it is the former, we should accept it with gratitude; when it is the latter, we should persevere undaunted. No matter how easy or how difficult it may be, we should regard it as a service to be faithfully performed. Contemplation is a good and beneficial force, and the whole of life is transformed when we practice it. Contemplation which is faithfully and painstakingly performed counts, on the whole, for more in the Christian life than contemplation that comes easily, and is rich in holy thoughts and the awareness of the presence of God.

Mystical prayer erases barriers between man and God

Finally we should like to discuss briefly a subject which goes beyond the scope of this book, but which is important enough to deserve some mention. It may happen in contemplation that we have a strange experience. We may have been reflecting on God in faith alone. Suddenly, God is present. This is not due to any intensity of devotion on our part, nor does it imply that we have an especially vivid idea of God or that our heart is overflowing with love for Him. It is not anything of this kind. It is a sudden feeling that we are faced with an entirely new and different experience: a wall which was there before is there no more.

Usually the idea of God is before us like everything else, including ourselves. It is before us in the space of our consciousness as a concept or thought. This concept of God affects us, moves us to love, or exhorts us to certain actions. In the experience which we are discussing, the barrier of thought disappears and gives place to immediate and direct awareness.

This, at first, may be most confusing. We feel moved in an entirely new way; we feel that we have been transported into a state hitherto unknown. Our intuition tells us that this is God or at any rate connected with Him. This intimation may frighten us. We do not know whether we dare presume that this intuition is true and we are uncertain what to do. However, the intuition becomes a certainty, even an absolute certainty which leaves no room for doubt. The doubts may come afterwards when, for example, we discover that our usual ideas about the inner life have lost their meaning or when we discover that other people have no knowledge of these things.

Another element of confusion is that we lack the words to describe our experience. We know what it is but we also know that it cannot be conveyed in words — not only because it is so great and powerful, but simply because there *is* no expression for it. We can merely say something like: "It is holy; it is close; it is more important than anything else; it is sufficient in itself; it is quiet, tender, simple; it is almost nothing and yet it is everything — it is He." We could put it this way, yet know that it would convey nothing to our listener unless he also had experienced it.

Mystical experience deepens and confirms faith

We know also that this holy event is beyond conscious control. No known power can bring the encounter about or direct it. We may have reached a very concentrated state of inner composure and pureness of mind, but whatever the degree of concentration or inner purification, this in itself can never bring about the advent of the Holy One. His coming is pure grace, and we ourselves can do no more than prepare ourselves and watch and pray.

What we have tried to sketch here is what the masters of the spiritual life call the *mystical vision*. The word *mystical* has been greatly abused; it has come to stand for everything which is mysterious or odd. In reality it has a precise meaning. It stands for a definite experience of God and of things divine. This experience may be accompanied by different manifestations, auditory or visual. Yet these are only byproducts which may even contain some element of risk; the less dramatic and sensational the experience is, the truer it is likely to be.

As to the significance and effect of such an experience, no general explanation is possible. It can mean, above all, a profound and inward reassurance of the reality of the living God and may become an infinitely precious aid to faith. Anyone who has undergone this experience may be able to say (with St. Paul), "I know to whom I have given my faith."[66] Once we have had this experience, we cannot easily forget that God exists and abides with us.

It also represents a challenge, calling man to a closer intimacy and partnership with God. It summons him to purify his life, to avoid with greater determination the entanglements of the world, and to turn himself wholeheartedly to God. At the same time it assures him of his ability to do so by giving him his own ground on which to stand and a source of power on which to draw.

Such an experience is also of importance to others, for it enables him who has been so blessed to bear witness. "I know that God lives," he is now able to say. Every doubt and objection he can counter with the weight of the words: "It *is* so — I have experienced it." Thus by bearing personal witness to God he may give others greater support.

Mystical experiences bring difficulties, blessings, and responsibilities

To people whose inner life is rich and full of sensibility, who are conscientious and take spiritual matters seriously, such a new element in their lives can be very disturbing. What are they to do?

[66]2 Tim. 1:12.

Above all they should guard and treasure it. The mystical experience of which we spoke awakens the longing to abide with Him who has thus declared Himself. Prayer, which hitherto may have been laborious, has suddenly become easy. Where words had been lacking, they now seem to come of their own accord — perhaps not many, perhaps only one, but always springing new from an inexhaustible source. In the face of this experience there awakens in man a profound, inward quality of which he himself was unaware; or one might say that, awakened by this experience, a lofty and remote side of himself suddenly comes to life.

He should therefore follow the call and pray with great sincerity. Simultaneously, he should observe moderation because his normal condition is changed and there is the danger that he might overstrain himself. Mystical experience may also bring other difficulties in its train, and these may be of a very acute kind. It may happen that things which had hitherto been important lose their significance and that people become strangely remote. It may happen that ordinary life becomes empty and that one feels lost in it, that one feels an urge to do something but without knowing exactly what. It may happen also that one doubts whether the whole experience had not merely been a delusion or temptation.

In the face of these difficulties and doubts one should remain calm and trust in God. One should submit to His will and pray for enlightenment, but until it comes one should endure the trial and proceed as usual. Thus faith is fortified and love becomes pure.

Mystical experience is true only if it stands the test to which apply the words: "By this is the Spirit of God known. Every spirit which confesseth that Jesus Christ is come in the flesh, is of God: and every spirit that dissolveth Jesus, is not of God."[67] Only that

---

[67] 1 John 4:2-3.

which stands the test before Christ is true before God. Thus we must bring such an experience first to Christ. We should say to ourselves, "All this I want only if Christ is there, if it is in His spirit, if it can hold its own before Him. Christ's name and His Cross is my standard; anything which is incompatible with that I do not want."

It may be tempting to abandon oneself to the divine in itself or to seek God as He is "beyond all words and ways," but there is great danger in this. At all times we must put the person of Christ into the center, refer to Him, think of Him, and commit everything into His hands.

Anyone who has been vouchsafed such an experience should realize the responsibilities it imposes. He will have to become stricter with himself, more conscientious in his duties, more careful in his prayer, more selective in his associates, his reading, and his recreations.

Furthermore, he will not talk lightly about these matters. It is always questionable whether one should discuss one's inner life; here it becomes doubly so, as it would mean discussing a secret which one shares with God. Moreover, any experience tends to become externalized by discussion, whereas in this particular case it is of paramount importance that it should remain inseparable from one's inmost experience.

Generally speaking, people will not easily talk about such experiences because they are so obviously sacred. At the same time, because they are so entirely new and different, sooner or later one will be compelled to speak about them, if only to put them to the test of words and prevent them from becoming a dream and a delusion in one's mind. One should seek out an experienced person and tell him everything. The advice of such a person should be taken seriously, while at the same time one should reserve the freedom to act according to one's own innermost conscience in case one has not been fully understood or one senses the danger of being unduly influenced.

The experience of which we speak is, like all living things, a seed capable of growth. This growth must go through various stages, each one bringing a new challenge and also probably new problems and upsets. A great deal more can be said about it which would, however, exceed the scope of this book. Here we merely wanted to indicate the problem because such experiences are on the whole more frequent than one would suspect. In an age of decline and disintegration such as ours, the inner sources seem to well up more abundantly and many a person whose outward life indicates nothing unusual may in fact have had such experiences. This is because they do not depend on individual talent or aptitude but on a grace given freely by God as He chooses.

6

Divine Providence

The Christian doctrine of Providence

In the message of Christ there is one doctrine — that of Divine Providence — which embraces the whole of existence and at the same time concerns each person individually. According to this, anything that happens in the world is directed by the love, wisdom, and might of the Father for the benefit of the faithful.

The word *Providence* is often used rather loosely with no more than a vague or ill-defined meaning. Therefore in the first place we must define its meaning. Christ has frequently spoken of Providence. He did so with special force and detail in the course of that body of teaching which is called the Sermon on the Mount.[68] There He admonishes His listeners to take no thought for food or raiment, for the heavenly Father knows what man

---

[68]Matt. 6:25-34.

needs. To worry about these things is to act like the heathen. The believer should have confidence that he will not lack anything.

The listener is not being asked to put his faith in a fairy tale. He is not being told that he can discard all labor and foresight and live heedlessly from day to day because miraculous powers will look after him.

What is being said takes into account life as it really is and overlooks none of its hardships. Providence is not therefore a flight of fancy but sober reality. On the other hand it is not something that should be taken for granted from a worldly point of view. For instance, Providence does not mean that everything follows an inviolable order in which one must find a place or that the self-confident can master life more easily than those who are anxious or distrustful. It means something quite out of this world — that the living God is personally concerned with every single human being and ready to look after him. Thus Providence is neither a fairy tale nor, on the other hand, a piece of natural philosophy; not a code of life but simply a revelation by the grace of God.

Providence calls us to seek first the kingdom of God

In the Sermon on the Mount, as an example of how God feels about the needs of His creatures, Christ points to the birds who neither sow nor reap and to the lilies of the field who neither toil nor spin. This, at first sight, would appear just a pious idyll, but then comes the sentence which shows how serious it all is: "Seek ye therefore first the kingdom of God, and His justice, and all these things shall be added unto you."[69]

[69]Matt. 6:33.

This sentence expresses what Christ means the proper attitude of God's children to be: that man should *first* seek the kingdom of God and His justice, that is, *before* and *more than* anything else. Man's concern about the kingdom should be the center and mainspring of his life.

This is something very great and very difficult which fundamentally assumes that conversion or repentance which the Lord demands at the beginning of His message: "Do penance, for the kingdom of heaven is at hand."[70]

Whoever thinks in this way is in agreement with God because he wishes that His kingdom and holy justice should come. Out of this understanding, Christ says, the course of events will fall into place around the faithful. Thus things, people, conditions, and destinies do not happen to us fortuitously but form a wholeness: the world of the individual. This wholeness differs according to the mentality and character of the person and, we may add, according to how far we allow for God's sway in our lives.

The course of events is not predetermined like the working of a machine but rather is infinitely fluid, full of potentialities, and ready to submit to the will which is able to govern it. A deeper insight into man shows to what an extent the inmost attitude, often quite unconsciously, determines the course of our destiny. Therefore, for the individual who is prepared to submit to the will of God, this destiny will be quite different from that of the man who acts according to his own obstinate and at the same time uncertain will.

Moreover — and this is the decisive factor — the world is in the hands of God. The laws of nature are His servants. Out of the hearts of men He orders the course of events, in each one of the

[70]Matt. 4:17.

individual worlds as well as in the world as a whole. Whenever, therefore, the human heart shares with Him the holy care for the kingdom, the word fulfills itself according to which "to them that love God, all things work together unto good."[71] This does not mean that the man who has submitted to the will of God will be spared pain and sorrow, but it does mean that he will have what he needs and that everything that happens, including the misfortunes, serves the true end of his life.

The message of Providence demands something very great of man: that he should make the care for God's kingdom the prime care of his life. It promises him something equally great: that the events which take place around him occur in a very special way and shape an existence which is determined by God's care for his particular good.

Faith helps us understand Providence

This promise is not a fairy tale but reality. But it is not that reality which is actually before us — in other words, a reality of nature or history — but the reality which springs from God. But again, it is not a kind of mysterious reality outside nature and history, but right in their midst. It is not apprehended, like a fairy tale, with our imagination, nor, on the other hand, like things of immediate actuality, by natural observation and intellect.

Providence is apprehended through the eyes of faith. We hear of it through the word of God; and having staked our faith on this reality we find it actually does come into being. The world, such as it is, always seems to contradict the working of Providence and our hearts are quickly perplexed and discouraged, so we must

[71]Rom. 8:28.

always renew our faith. Slowly we begin to see the underlying pattern — for instance, the meaning of an event, of an encounter, of a success or a failure.

We sense behind the forces and necessities which otherwise govern events a new power and a new purpose. We feel that we are included in a holy design which comes from God.

This awareness may at times become very vivid and then again disappear. Often it will pervade our life merely as a feeling of quiet confidence. For the rest, it will be based on faith. The ultimate remains hidden and will be revealed only when, at the end of time, the kingdom of God is fulfilled. That which happens by Providence in the life of the individual is a part and an aspect of the coming world, in which, on a new earth and under a new heaven, the new man will live.[72] This world is already in process of emerging around those who open themselves to Providence, but it will be revealed only at the end of all things.

Contemplative prayer reveals the workings of Providence

In the world of the New Testament, Christian consciousness is steeped in the idea of Divine Providence, and with unsophisticated people whose lives are — or appear to be — governed by forces entirely beyond their control, this is still to a certain extent true today.

But, generally speaking, faith in Divine Providence does not now play an important part in Christian life. There are many causes for this which we cannot discuss here, but undoubtedly a more active faith in Providence should be an essential factor in the Christian life and, for that matter, also in Christian prayer.

[72]Rev. 21:1.

Above all we should reflect on Divine Providence in order to understand and to absorb its meaning. We have talked about contemplation — one of its most fruitful subjects should be the message of Divine Providence, especially the words of our Lord on this subject, not only in the great passage in the Sermon on the Mount, but also His other utterances, teachings, and parables throughout the Gospels. We should also contemplate Christ's own relationship to the will of the Father, that experience which He called His "hour,"[73] the way in which He experienced and underwent events, and the temper of His mind.

Then we must learn to understand the world and history in the context of Providence, overcoming the concept of an impersonal, mechanistic world order which has been forced upon us by science and is reflected in the attitude of the masses. This conception is false. By it, the world is taken out of the hands of God, but it does not thereby acquire an independent scientific or cultural status, but passes into the hands of God's enemy. Thus the task is, by contemplation, to draw the world back into its true focus. The doctrine of Providence runs counter to the general trend of opinion. Here we must hold our ground. It is the battle of faith whose victory "overcomes the world"[74] — the old unregenerate world — and ushers in the new, eternal one.

Contemplation reveals what God demands of us in this moment

In the Sermon on the Mount there is the Lord's Prayer. Its true meaning becomes clear only in the light of the doctrine of Providence. Not until we recognize that it is the living God who governs the destiny of the world and evaluate the meaning of our

[73]John 2:4; 7:30; 12:27.
[74]John 16:33.

132

own individual existence under this aspect — and, even more, not until we also understand that the kingdom of God is entrusted to our care, weak and insufficient as we are — will we grasp the full import of the Lord's Prayer.

We are not so much concerned here with the wider implications of Providence as with God's governance as it is fulfilled from event to event in the life of the individual. Thus it is the task of contemplation to try to grasp the pattern of this life and the meaning of specific phases and situations in the light of Divine Providence.

This Providence does not unfold according to a fixed program but works through the facts and developments in our lives. The streams of general and personal existence flow together. Irresistibly conditions change and causes act, phenomena appear and disappear. At the same time something strange happens: the flow of events assumes an order around us and seems to pose a challenge. "Look," it appears to say, "understand, act, do what is required at this moment for the coming of the kingdom, for if you fail to do it now, it can never be done again." This is the situation, "the hour," my hour, in which the will of God becomes concrete for me. This is the situation which I make part of my contemplation and try to understand. "What does it mean in the sight of God? What is my part in it?"

God demands something of me which belongs to "His kingdom and its righteousness."[75] He demands it of me and He demands it now. He will enable me to understand what this is. "How?" we might ask. We obtain this understanding not through mystical experience or illumination but through the truth inherent in the situation. The truth of this situation will be revealed as soon as we

[75]Matt. 6:33; Luke 12:31.

133

cease to regard it from the point of view of the world or our own self-will, but take it to God, ready to submit it to His judgment.

The uncertainty about what to do may spring from various sources. For instance, the situation may not as yet present a clear challenge and one cannot therefore know what is the right course: in this case one should not act but wait. Or vision and judgment may be lacking, in which case one should do one's best according to one's lights. The obscurity may be due to the fact that man is not in agreement with God; his own will pits itself against the manifest will of God, blinding vision and blurring judgment.

As soon as he has convinced himself that the will of God is right and salutary, and he has made himself free and ready to act upon it, the uncertainties vanish — although not necessarily all those which come merely from the unripeness of the situation or the incapacity of understanding or judgment, but those which arise from the resistance of the will.

God's Providence is fulfilled through our actions

The moral judgments of the modern Christian are based on a set of standards and a system of values. Although this is right as far as it goes, there is always the danger that it may become a mere philosophy and thereby lose its connection with God's free rule in Providence. The life of mankind as well as of the individual does not unfold according to a set of standards which have to be observed or a system of values to be realized, but God Himself is at work deciding, creating, and acting everywhere, including in ourselves. My life is a point — the point which concerns me — where God acts, the workshop in which He creates. From me something new is meant to emerge.

Christian conduct is man acting in harmony with the activity of God: acting with humility because God alone matters, with obedience because from this activity should emerge something which can emerge only through God, and at the same time acting with lively confidence because every individual is a starting-point for the divine creation.

Undoubtedly the standards of ethics and Christian morality, the tenets of Christian faith, and the rules of the Church are binding. At the same time we must not forget that there are things which cannot be gathered from rules and regulations but only from the day-to-day situation as it emerges from God. Being in each case something new, something unique, they cannot be labeled or classified and yet they constitute at least one half of our existence.

This attitude will strengthen something which in many people has become extremely weak — namely, a Christian conscience. What we usually mean by this is the awareness that the moral law is binding and the capacity of judging how it should be applied in the individual case.

This conception loses sight of one whole side of existence: the feeling for the demands of the hitherto unknown, the capacity to visualize what will happen, the courage to perform that for which there is no example.

All that is part of conscience. But if we fail to see it, something strange happens to our moral life; it becomes monotonous and boring and it may lead (especially in those who are high-spirited) to rebellion, quite apart from the fact that much good remains undone and many noble impulses go to waste.

The idea of Providence and faith in it are able to awaken that unused side of conscience, and to give it a proper foundation and stability. Left to itself it might prove a breeding ground of rebellion and arbitrariness. This danger is overcome by making ourselves aware that we are not acting, as it were, privately and on our own, but in an allotted place within the wholeness of God's plan, standing in His sight and accountable to Him.

We must offer ourselves to be instruments of Providence

In the light of these considerations, prayer becomes the request that God may fulfill His holy Providence in the life of the worshipper. "Thy will be done on earth as it is in heaven," says the Lord's Prayer. This will is directed to the coming of the kingdom and the coming of the new earth. Thus prays the man who shares with God the care that His will may be done not only in the general course of history but in his own individual life.

If this request is to be serious, it must mean that the worshipper holds himself at the disposal of the holy plan, declaring himself willing to do his share and to take upon himself everything that this involves, even though it be very onerous.

The will of God for His kingdom does not work itself out in accordance with the limitations which He has imposed upon Himself in the laws of nature governing the growth of trees and the course of the stars, but in the fullness of freedom. Thus man in prayer must will the coming of the kingdom. Herein lies the gravity of being a Christian: the inescapability of the call, in which no one can take another's place because everyone has his appointed part.

We must constantly pray for guidance

Out of this awareness arises the prayer that God may show us what we should do. Here it is not a matter of fixed rules which we must acknowledge and carry out, but of concrete realities which must be understood in the context of divine action and of the reality not yet in being for which man is responsible and in which he must play his part. Thus we must ask God to give us eyes to see. "It is a great grace to be allowed to see," says the poet, and this is true. The will of God may be revealed in everything around us, but we do not see it because our eyes are held down. They are held down by weakness, sloth, cowardice, and self-seeking. They can be opened only from within, from that innermost ground accessible to God alone.

Equally, it is an infinite grace to see "what is not yet" — not the irrelevant or the fantastic, but that which concerns us and can come into being only by our doing. This may be small or great: the good of a person entrusted to our care or a thought which is destined one day to influence the whole world. We must therefore ask God to draw the attention of our hearts to the call of the yet unrealized.

Even greater than the grace of understanding is the grace of putting into effect, by which the will is strengthened and made patient so that it may persevere through all difficulties in its endeavors.

Prayer is also the best opportunity for learning the acid test of faith in Providence, namely the acceptance of difficulty and pain. As long as things go our way or troubles are experienced merely as obstacles that strengthen our resolve, it is easy enough to believe that everything is being guided by providential love.

The greatness of the demand becomes apparent when our vision and will are left in the dark and there seems to be no sense or meaning in what is happening. This is the time for the victory of our faith, which conquers the world. That faith puts its trust in the word of God that everything which happens is within His Providence even though we cannot feel it. It maintains that behind the apparent confusion there is a plan, behind loss a gain which cannot yet be recognized, and that through all trouble something valid is developing. This "yes" to God's wisdom and power is learnt in prayer. By constant attempts the heart sincerely, generously, and courageously practices this affirmation to the mysterious working of God's love.

Prayer links the supernatural to the historical

It has been said that Christian prayer is not suited to modern man and that he has outgrown it. True, there have been people in all ages who have advanced this argument, when it would have been more honest to say that man did not want to pray. But all the same there is some truth in this assertion. Christian prayer has to a large extent lost contact with life as it now is. For instance, it is said with some justification that prayer has become a passive affair of concern only to women, while man, whose nature it is to act, can have little part in it.

Throughout the ages women's share in prayer has played an important part. When it is revealed at the Last Judgment what has worked in the whole of existence as well as in individual lives, when it is revealed who were the sustained and who the sustainers, what has been preserved and what would have been confused without such protection, then it will be seen how much of man's struggling and striving was made possible by the hidden prayers of women. Life as a whole — the attitude which determines it, the mentality which carries it, the matters which concern it, the words which it uses — is frequently influenced by women in a manner in which men cannot share.

Fundamentally, too, the normal woman cannot exercise this kind of influence because in the relationship between a man and a woman, if one dominates the other in the wrong way, the essential character of each is spoilt. If the feminine aspect is suppressed, the masculine degenerates into the purely male. If, on the other hand, the man ceases to play a part in any particular sphere of life, the woman becomes merely female. The same sort of disturbance of balance has overtaken prayer.

It often appears that prayer is shunning active participation in life and, having withdrawn into a sphere of its own, is concerned only with otherworldly matters. The future of Christian life depends, among other things, on whether prayer can establish an active link with life as it is and with the stream of history. Here, again, the idea of Providence is the starting-point. In such a conception of prayer, man has as important a place as woman.

We must pray that God's will may be done

In this context prayer for others assumes its proper meaning. Its most immediate form is making specific requests — for example, that the sick may be well again, that a professional difficulty may be solved, that a threatening disaster may be averted, and so forth. But these are only the outward manifestations of something far more profound. The illness, for example, does not stand by itself, but has its place in the life history of the particular individual. Thus prayer becomes right only if we implore God to fulfill in this illness His providential will over that person and to help him to reach that understanding, undergo that test, or reach that maturity which is meant to come to him through the illness.

The prayer that God's will be done therefore does not mean that the inevitable should be fulfilled and that we are prepared to resign ourselves to it. The will of God is not a fate which has to be endured, but a holy and meaningful act which ushers in a new creation. The demand is that the work should be fulfilled in the way which helps that creation most.

This is as true for the world as a whole as for the individual. The course of the world would be very different if the faithful offered up events to God in the right kind of prayer — and not only with the intent that He should help in this matter or prevent that emergency — but that the great work of His will and the glory of His kingdom should come to the earthly fulfillment that is meant for it here and now.

According to the degree of insight, this prayer will demand something specific, but apart from that it will consist in man "seeking the kingdom of God and its righteousness," carrying in his heart the care for the coming of the kingdom and thus creating there a space of realization and an opening for the will of God to pour into the world.

The externals succeed only if they are supported from within. The world can exist only if it is somewhere known, lived, and suffered in the spirit. This quiet, secret space which the world in its noisy arrogance does not consider, whose existence it ignores, is being hewn by prayer out of Providence.

We should remain constant in prayer

The spiritual masters say that prayer should gradually extend from the short time in which it is explicitly practiced to the whole day. They remind us of the words of the Lord that we ought "always to pray, and not to faint."[76]

This refers, in the first place, to the earnestness with which the believer calls to the Father for help until his prayer is answered. But beyond this it refers to the constancy of prayer in general, through which his prayers should develop from a specific practice to an intrinsic part of his life and from an act to an attitude or state of being.

The justification for this is perhaps not easily understood. It presumes that the inner life has already reached a certain degree of development and that conversation with God has become very dear to the heart. This, however, one cannot force. Thus one should not propose to do anything for which the time is not right.

[76]Luke 18:1.

In spiritual matters zeal is important but circumspection, which knows how to wait until the time is ripe, is equally so.

We must learn to make our life itself a prayer

Once man has understood that prayer is not an exceptional state but a permanent element of an existence which is directed toward God, he will extend it to every aspect of his daily life. There are different ways of doing this.

There is, above all, the contemplative approach. It originates in the act of prayer itself and consists in introducing certain elements of contemplation into the routine of daily life. For instance, if we frequently recollect ourselves and establish the consciousness of the presence of God, a series of *stations of prayer* will be set up in the course of the day which will draw closer and closer together. Or from contemplation with its explicit focusing on God we may develop a general attitude of reverence which permeates the day's activity, imparting to it a religious character. Out of this gradually develops what is called "moving in the presence of God" or "life in the sight of God."

But we can also make the idea of Providence our starting-point. We can, as it were, live ourselves into this conception and thus establish an intimate contact with God's rule and a permanent consciousness or feeling that God is at work in every event. If in the course of the day we think again and again of this living, tender, yet mighty mystery, or feel it, this becomes a true act of prayer, which we can extend to any length we desire. In so doing, we need not turn aside from the normal activities of life because it is just in these activities that the prayer takes place. We receive what happens as coming from the Father and offer our own work up to Him — making it part of His work. We see ourselves in a holy association with Him in the light of which we understand our life from hour to hour. In this armor we can stand forth boldly in the world.

Here life itself becomes prayer. This can bring many profound experiences. Thus St. Augustine tells in the ninth book of his *Confessions* how he had once suffered from an intense pain and had been delivered from it by his prayer. "But what kind of pain was it? Or how did it leave me? I was startled, I admit, my Lord and God, for I had never experienced anything of the kind in all my life and deep in my heart I understood Thy sign and, rejoicing in faith, glorified Thy name."[77]

The emotion which even today lives in these words does not spring from the intensity of the pain or its startling relief but from the saint's experience, in a context of pain, prayer, and liberation, of God's providential act. It was as if he had been transported to the center of existence of which before he had known only the outer aspect or, at best, had had the merest inkling. Nothing very special had happened. Pain is a daily occurrence, and there may be many reasons for its disappearance. But in all this he had experienced the mysterious working of Providence. In it the ordinary daily events suddenly become hints and signs which we understand deep in our hearts and to which we respond with adoration and praise. Such an experience, however, is an extraordinary event and is granted by God's special favor; it shows the luminous goal of the road which the faithful should tread.

We should offer our lives and suffering to God

Even when we were children we were told that we should, at the beginning of the day and frequently during it, make the "good

---

[77]St. Augustine, *Confessions*, Bk. 9, Ch. 4, Para. 12.

"resolution" that all our actions should be to the glory of God. The meaning and value of any action ultimately depends on what is intended — that is to say, on the motive and mentality from which it springs. The intention changes from time to time with the alertness and purity of our state of mind and with the character of the object.

Thus we have been admonished that the whole course of our life should be dedicated indeflectibly — by an explicit act of resolve — to the greater glory of God. Everything, even the most ordinary and insignificant action, can serve this greater glory, as St. Paul puts it in the First Epistle to the Corinthians: "Therefore, whether you eat or drink, or whatsoever else you do, do all to the glory of God."[78]

In the passage leading to these words St. Paul discusses whether one is permitted to eat certain foods. He brings this matter to a conclusion by saying that such distinctions are of relative unimportance compared with the supreme demand that the whole of life with everything that happens should be a holy service performed before the majesty of God.

By the good resolution our intention should be constantly redirected toward God and the resulting action offered up to Him as a just due. One should not object to this by saying that such an act is contrived and artificial, for what St. Paul had in mind was the basic attitude of the faithful, which should determine everything, both great and small. No doubt, to make the good resolution could be called something *contrived* — contrived, however, in the sense of an act of the will which has been mentioned several times in the course of this book. The examining, ordering, and uplifting of our actions to God must, to begin with, be consciously willed

[78] 1 Cor. 10:31.

143

until it gradually becomes second nature and can in due course determine our conduct.

The right way to offer ourselves to God

All the same, the way in which this conception should be formulated and put into practice needs to be given some thought. Frequently the so-called ordering of our actions toward God takes very little account of what this really means but merely consists in giving to the action — provided of course it is morally good or at least unobjectionable — a label "To the Glory of God" (rather in the nature of a mathematical sign).

But does not this show a certain disregard for the true essence of the action? The glory of God is not served by doing something merely as a duty or at least to avoid sin, and then offering it up to God, but rather by doing right for its own sake and for what would seem to be God's own reasons, in the way in which circumstances demand and conscience approves, as men have a right to expect and in accordance with tact, friendship, love, loyalty, and honor. What is thus right in itself is brought by that same dedication before the Creator, the Lord of all things.

There exists, however, a mentality which would overlook the essential rightness of an action and maintain that, as long as no sin is committed, what is being done is fundamentally a matter of indifference. According to this view, what really matters is that the letter of the law should be obeyed and that this obedience should be inspired by the right intention. This may be appropriate at certain moments of the spiritual life when, for instance, the striving toward objectivity has tempted man to set himself up as the ultimate judge of his conduct. Generally speaking, however, this sort of mentality destroys the responsibility which the Creator has imposed on man toward His creation.

By this we do not mean, of course, that achievement as such is the measure of our action in the sight of God. If this were so, only the most highly gifted would be capable of serving Him — quite apart from the fact that no human achievement can claim to be noteworthy in the eyes of God.

What ultimately determines the value of our action is the intention or motive behind it, whether the results are commensurate with this or not.

The intention, however, must not disregard the action itself. On the contrary, we must see to it, to the best of our ability, that the action is both appropriate and sensible. A good deed does not consist in meaning the right thing and doing it just anyhow, but rather it consists in our doing it as well as we can and in our obedience to the will of the Creator as it is expressed in the laws of the world.

Providence presents to the individual, in the form of an overall situation, those people, conditions, and circumstances which are important to him at that moment, and demands of him that he should act — not on an abstract principle nor, on the other hand, with subjective arbitrariness, but in accordance with the demands inherent in the situation itself.

To recognize God's will in the challenge of a situation and to comply with it in the appropriate way is truly doing everything to His greater glory.

If, then, the "practice of the good resolution" rests on such foundations, it is endowed with a new depth, and the element of fortuitousness and irrelevance in "everything to the greater glory of God" disappears. The intention to act to the glory of God combines with the responsibility toward His will inherent in the order of reality and the challenge of the situation; thus the action becomes that of a man who is conscious of his responsibility for the care of God's kingdom.

God continually transforms creation

It is frequently said that Christianity must regain more of its eschatological character. The *eschata* — the last things — are the things which happen at the end of time: the second coming of Christ, His judgment, the end of the world, and the beginning of the new creation. *Eschatological* is an attitude in which those last things come into their own. Thus not only does the believer know that the world and history will one day come to an end and that, when everything is submitted to the judgment of Christ, eternity will be in accordance with this judgment; the believer will also realize that that which will one day be revealed openly has now already begun, hidden and denied though it still be. This also means that everything in existence now does not yet have its true form. What people and things really are will be revealed when our Lord returns. Everything happens with a view to that event, enclosed, enshrined, in the message of Revelation. "Dearly beloved, we are now the sons of God; and it hath not yet appeared what we shall be. We know that, when He shall appear, we shall be like to Him: because we shall see Him as He is."[79]

> For I reckon that the sufferings of this time are not worthy to be compared with the glory to come, that shall be revealed in us. For the expectation of the creature waiteth for the revelation of the sons of God. For the creature was made subject to vanity, not willingly, but by reason of him that made it subject, in hope: Because the creature also itself shall be delivered from the servitude of corruption, into the liberty of the glory of the children of God. For we know that every creature groaneth and travaileth in pain, even until

[79] 1 John 3:2.

now. And not only it, but ourselves also, who have the first fruits of the Spirit, even we ourselves groan within ourselves, waiting for the adoption of the sons of God, the redemption of our body. For we are saved by hope. But hope that is seen, is not hope. For what a man seeth, why doth he hope for? But if we hope for that which we see not, we wait for it with patience.[80]

The world which is seemingly so clearly defined, distinct, sure, and so utterly concrete, is in fact none of these things; in it God is effecting a constant process of transformation. Under cover of the old, in day-to-day events, encounters, and actions, grows the new world, which will be completed at the second coming of Christ. True eschatological feeling consists in bearing the idea of this process in mind and carrying it as a solace and inner strength, putting oneself in contact with the all-permeating mystery of divine government.

[80]Rom. 8:18-25.

7

Prayer to the Saints
and to the Mother of God

Our relation to the saints

The life of man is realized in various kinds of mutual relationships. No one stands by himself alone: everyone depends on others, giving and taking, influencing and being influenced. As we hope that the departed live in God, we must believe that this applies to them, too — for surely that which is one of the most essential parts of life cannot have come to an end for them.

As a matter of fact the Christian has a lively consciousness of his connection with those departed who were linked to him by blood-relationship, love, or spiritual affinity. He hopes for a reunion with them in the life to come; he thinks of the purification which they may have to undergo to attain "the glorious liberty of the children of God."[81]

---

[81]Rom. 8:21.

The idea, however, of appealing to their love on his own behalf hardly ever occurs to him. He may feel the need to prove himself to them, or that he is bound to carry out some instruction which they have given. But beyond that he feels that the gulf of death is too great and that the religious stature of the departed is, on the whole, not sufficient for him to invoke their spiritual aid in any real sense of the word.

It is different when we come to people whose lives were filled with God's spirit in a very special way. We read that from the earliest times the faithful have asked the martyrs (that is to say, those who bore witness to God by their own blood) for their intercession — perhaps even during their lifetime (for instance, in prison or on the way to execution) but above all after their death. And they did this, not out of a fortuitous impulse of religious sentiment, but in keeping with the very heart of the Liturgy — the holy Mass. In early times it became a custom to erect altars above the tombs of the martyrs and their invocation was included in the prayer of the Mass.

This is true for saints generally. The term *saint* has changed greatly in the course of the centuries. In the New Testament it included all those who believed in Christ, who were reborn by Baptism, and stood in the communion of the Eucharist — in other words, all Christians. However, with the growing number of the faithful, the meaning of the word *saint* was narrowed down, and more and more was used to denote something exceptional, which revealed itself (through the call and guidance of God) in the form of an absolute devotion and in greatness of experience and action in certain individuals.

Such people as Martin of Tours, Augustine, Francis of Assisi, Catherine of Siena, Elizabeth of Thuringia, Teresa of Avila, all lived on earth subject to the necessities and the insufficiency of human existence like everyone else; at the same time they were living witnesses of another world and were filled with its mystery. They truly put into effect the commandment to love God with all their heart, and with all their soul, and with all their strength, and with all their mind, and their neighbors as themselves — thus living not for themselves but for the whole of mankind.[82] So man when he appealed to them in his distress felt that he was recognized and received as nowhere else.

Love between human beings can be very great. For example, a father works himself to the bone for his children or a mother devotes her whole life to them. Yet much of this love is simply the tie of blood and instinct; only gradually and through much struggle does it rise above these natural limits. The love of the saints arises from a selflessness which comes from God alone and which, with holy earnestness, desires the good of others. Is it not right, therefore, that we should continue to seek this love, even after the hearts in which it lived have ceased to beat on earth?

Death according to Christian belief is not an end but a transition. Those who die in the name of Christ do not enter into the void but into the fullness of holy reality.

Man instinctively believes that the dead become shadowy and shrinks away from them to seek the warm light of the earthly sun, or he may believe that the dead become an uncanny or destructive influence against which he must seek protection. These instinctive feelings are overcome by faith, which teaches us that those who died in a state of grace have attained to the glorious liberty of the children of God and the pure fulfillment of their being in eternal light. Is it not appropriate, therefore, that we should seek in their glorious liberty those who even while on earth were witnesses of divine love and power?

[82]Mark 12:30-31.

The saints reflect the majesty of God

This, therefore, is how it has come about that from the earliest days of Christianity there has existed a living relationship between the faithful and those who, while on earth, proved themselves the friends of God in a very special way — namely, the saints. This relationship has many different aspects.

At first sight, it seems to consist almost entirely in the appeal for help, an invocation fully justified because the predicament of existence is very grave. Thus to seek the love of those who have fully entered into communion with God, who are at one with His will and filled with His grace, is a natural expression of the life of faith. But in addition to the appeal, praise takes a prominent place, rejoicing at the devout and noble lives of the saints, their deeds and victory, and at the divine guidance manifested in them. They are the witnesses to redemption.

The *new creation* which constantly re-emerges from Christ is hidden; everything seems to belie it and faith has great difficulty in retaining its conviction that it will one day be accomplished. The saints, radiant in the glorious liberty of the children of God, encourage us in this hope.

They may also assume a special responsibility for the manner in which the individual conducts his life. They open up the riches of Christ. Whereas He is "the Light,"[83] simple and at the same time all-embracing, the saints break up this mysterious brilliance like a prism breaking up the white light in the spectrum, allowing first one color to shine and then another. They can help the believer to understand himself in this light of Christ and to discover the road which leads to Him.

[83] John 8:12.

The profoundest motive, however, which leads us toward the saints is the desire simply to be in their company — to abide with them. It is love seeking the communion of those who have dedicated their lives to love and who are now fulfilled in it; it is the desire for that holy atmosphere in which the soul can breathe and for the mysterious current which nourishes it; it is the longing for the answer to the ultimate meaning of existence.

It is all this, in the final analysis, which the believer seeks from the saints, although at first sight it may appear that what matters to him is their help. In a closer scrutiny of the lives of certain Christians we may be impressed by the discovery of a close connection with a saint.

The relationship to the saints is wholesome and fundamentally natural and right. Admittedly, they were only human beings, but they have entered into the mystery of God and the new creation is completed in them. The believer does not seek in them great personalities, but rather God's witnesses in whom God has been fulfilled. This veneration may at times assume undue proportions. In the lives of some people, or at certain times, it may almost displace God. Of course, much depends on how we look at it. The prejudiced may, in some individual case, easily assume that God has been displaced when the unprejudiced would clearly understand that God's holiness is the only real object of veneration. On the other hand, the proper order may really be upset and Christian conscience be forced to protest. Let us remind ourselves here of the words of the *Gloria: "Tu solus Sanctus: Tu solus Dominus: Tu solus Altissimus, Jesu Christe, cum Sancto Spiritu, in gloria Dei Patris"* ("For Thou only art holy; Thou only art the Lord; Thou only, O Jesus Christ, with the Holy Spirit, art most high in the glory of God the Father").

The prayer of the individual and of the community alike must be dominated by the majesty of God. It is He who must be adored and glorified; it is before Him that we must confess our sins. It is His grace that we must invoke. To Him we must give thanks at all times and everywhere so as to allow for no obscurity as to the aim and object of Christian prayer. Veneration of the saints then assumes its right place and proportion.

Love of the saints draws us to God

It may be most important for an individual to become particularly close to one or another among the great number of saints. As we have said, the saints show us the way to Christ. From each one of them radiates certain elements of His infinitely rich and, at the same time, simple plenitude, which thus becomes especially discernible to us. The saints are the explorers in the kingdom of God, the discoverers of His magnitude and power. Thus they blaze a trail which others can tread and they create a way of life which others, who could not have created it for themselves, can also adopt. A saint who is spiritually linked to us may truly become a guide and teacher; such a relationship is, or at least can be, completely mutual. We have reminded ourselves already that the saints do not live merely in books and pictures but in reality. They love those who are joined with them in Christ; and so from this union of a common love there is no knowing what contacts and relationships may spring.

There is a form of zeal for God which contains destructive elements. To make sure that nothing can compete with God it tries, as it were, to exterminate everything around Him which has a sacred character. The Gospels relate a strange incident in the life of our Lord, in which Jesus speaks to the Pharisees — the zealots for the honor of the one God — who are angered because He claimed a position which was, in their opinion, derogatory to this honor. They wanted to stone him, claiming that He was making

Himself God. Jesus answered them: " 'Is it not written in your law: "I said you are gods?" ' If he [the poet of Psalm 81] called them gods, to whom the word of God was spoken, and the Scripture cannot be broken; do you say of Him whom the Father hath sanctified and sent into the world: 'Thou blasphemest,' because I said: 'I am the Son of God'? "[84]

This is revealing. The opponents of Jesus are zealous for the honor of God but in a manner which surrounds His generosity with a wall. They rage against everything which, in their opinion, challenges God's uniqueness — with the result that the triune life of God, as revealed in Christ, is branded as a blasphemy. We are quoting this merely by way of illustration of a misplaced jealousy for God. Our own point of emphasis is altogether different. There is only one God and all honor is His. He has allowed the light of His holiness to shine in those who have fully merged with Christ's love — in every one of them according to his or her own measure and character. This may provoke the same type of pharisaical outburst which we saw in the Gospel story, and misplaced zeal for God's honor may impose arbitrary restrictions on His generosity. True piety is aware of the uniqueness of God but at the same time may love and honor the revelations of His grace as manifested in His saints.

The unique role and dignity of Mary

Among those invoked in Christian prayer Mary, the mother of our Lord, holds a very special place. She is not merely the greatest of the saints but something altogether different and unique. Volumes have been said and written about her. Much of this is very

[84]John 10:33-36.

beautiful and springs from the purest sources of Christian faith, but a great deal is of doubtful value. We must therefore try to be a little discriminating.

If one tries to explain wherein lies the special character and dignity of Mary, one can hardly do better than state the simple truth that she is the mother of the Redeemer: not only the mother of the man Jesus into whom, according to the Gnostics, the *Logos* entered, but of Jesus Christ, who is both God and Man. "And the angel answering, said to her: 'The Holy Spirit shall come upon thee, and the power of the Most High shall overshadow thee. And therefore also the Holy which shall be born of thee shall be called the Son of God.' "[85] That infant which was the fulfillment of Mary's destiny as a woman was to become her Redeemer and ours. What more can be said? By becoming a mother, she became Christian. By living for her child, she grew to full Christian stature. Her life is linked to the life of the Redeemer not only as every man who loves Him is linked to Him, but also as a mother to her son. She took part in His life. The Gospel tells us vividly how she followed Him even to the foot of the Cross, faithful in the truest sense of the word.

The Son of God was incarnate of the Virgin Mary by the Holy Spirit and was made man. In that hour the moving principle of creation held sway, not by commanding "Let there be," as it did when it created the world, but through the hearts and minds of those whom it called to fulfill its design. The message of the angel was at the same time an announcement, a demand, and a question. To this the answer was given in humility and obedience but also in freedom. The event which signified for all humanity the coming of the Redeemer and for the world the beginning of the new

---

[85] Luke 1:35.

156

creation, also signified for Mary the entry into her own unique relationship with God. The life, Passion, death, and Resurrection of our Lord, which are, for all, the guarantee and the beginning of salvation, were at the same time for her the true end of her personal life. By contributing toward salvation in this unique way, she herself reached the fullness of Christian perfection.

Christians rightly venerate Mary

When Mary, after the death of her Son, stayed with John, the faithful must have sought her out and asked her to tell them about Christ. Was she not the only one who could bear witness to the first thirty years of His life? To her the Holy Spirit had come and had made her understand the mystery of that life and the ultimate meaning of that which she, without comprehending the greatness of God, had "kept . . . in her heart."[86] Thus through the Holy Spirit she attained a unique knowledge of Christ.

If anybody wanted to know who Christ had been, the Apostles could give the authoritative answer. But there was also another answer which came from the knowledge derived from the community of a shared life, from purity of heart, and from the depths of a mother's love. Thus inevitably people came to her saying: "Tell us of your Son." Again one can never estimate how much of her words have entered into the Gospel story. For one thing, the disciples must have learnt many details from her which only she could have known; but beyond this, her intimate knowledge must have thrown a new light on events which were already known.

One cannot fail to imagine that people came to her with their problems, asking her to remember them in her prayers. They must

[86]Luke 2:51.

have seen how closely she was linked to her Son, waiting for the hour when He would call her to Himself. No doubt one person and another said to her: "Think of me in your prayers." So it has been ever since. The history of piety bears rich testimony to this; and anyone who is able to look at the figure of the Virgin in poetry and the arts from more than a purely aesthetic point of view frequently sees in it the expression of the highest Christian devotion.

From earliest days, the trust of the Christians had given her the name *Mother*. Was she not the mother of Jesus and He "the firstborn amongst many brethren"?[87] Did it not follow, therefore, that the love which she had for her Son must be available also to His brethren? The early Christians also knew (from the Gospel stories of the message of the angel and the care of Joseph her betrothed) that her motherhood was surrounded by the luster of virginity.[88] Thus the Church has seen in her the realization of the unity of virginal and motherly womanhood and fulfillment of one of the most ancient notions of the human race. In veneration of Mary, trust in the inexhaustibility of motherly love combines with reverent awe before her virginal sublimity. She is both near and distant, closely linked to us and at the same time infinitely remote.

Christians rightly meditate on the life of Mary

It is difficult to say in a few words what brings the believer to Mary. Many come to seek her help. Mary is called the "Comforter of the Afflicted," "Help of Christians," "Mother of Good Counsel." In her, the mother of the Redeemer, the believer experiences an inexhaustible compassion for all distress and affliction. She is the chosen one of God, lifted up to Him, not as a goddess living in

[87]Rom. 8:29.
[88]Luke 1:34; Matt. 1:18, 25.

the bliss of her exalted nature, but holding a unique position in the scheme of redemption by the grace of Christ. For this reason the Christian believer knows that he can be sure of her love.

One cannot overestimate what this means to man, that he can bring all his sorrows — even the most hidden and unspoken — into the span of such a love. And so the prayers of the afflicted constantly rise to her asking for help. Not that she can help us by her own power: neither Mary nor the saints can act on their own, for in God's kingdom, His will alone exists. Admittedly, the dead reach fulfillment and become masters of their own innermost selves, but they do so only in God, and their personal wills desire nothing but that His will may be done. Therefore, the help they can give to human affliction happens entirely by the will of God. The Church expresses this by saying that the saints intercede for us. The prayers of the afflicted call to Mary for this intercession, knowing that they will be answered.

As important as the invocation for help is joy over this heavenly figure so beloved of God and over that existence supported by such great faith and filled with such a profound mystery. For this reason there are in the veneration of Mary elements both of contemplation and of joyful praise. These find expression in many forms of devotion and in poetry, music, sculpture, and painting.

The ultimate motive which leads the believer to Mary is, as already said, the desire to be within the orbit of her holy life. The believer desires to dwell in her proximity, in the aura of her being, and in the intimacy of her mystery. The word *mystery* does not stand here for a riddle in the sense of something still unsolved. It conveys rather a quality, a potentiality, a sphere: the governance of God in man, the breath of eternal life. Here the worshipper wants to enter; here he wants to dwell, to breathe, to become quiet, and to receive comfort and strength to continue his life with renewed courage.

These various motives combine in a peculiar fashion in the Rosary, which was discussed earlier. The Rosary contains the ever renewed appeal for the intercession of Mary which is capable of embracing all the sorrows that afflict human life. It includes meditation upon that God-filled existence and participation in and rejoicing over its riches. It brings also a restful abiding in her presence. At the same time the Rosary brings out the true significance of the figure of the Virgin, because the focus of all such meditation is the part which she played in the life of Christ.

Excesses have interfered with proper veneration of Mary

The veneration of Mary is right and proper from a Christian point of view and it was not a happy hour when people thought that for the sake of Christ's honor they had to minimize His intimate link with His mother.

This, of course, did not come about purely by accident. Man has a tendency to exaggerate what he loves and in this way a good deal of extravagance, not to say fantasy, entered into his relationship with Mary. Add to this the influence of legend, and the instinct of the people to invest the figures of those dear to them with extraordinary attributes and to fill their lives with miraculous events. Finally, there is a tendency toward sentimentality and mawkishness. All this was bound to lead to abuse in connection with the veneration of Mary. It is not surprising, therefore, that criticism of every kind, justified and unjustified, has arisen and that many serious minds have been unable to find a way to Mary. They have tried to disassociate themselves from the exaggerations and deviations but, unable to distinguish the wheat from the chaff, have thrown all away. This is a thousand pities because the history of Christian piety shows how well the true veneration of Mary accords with the most vivid conception of Christian truth.

8

Prayer in Times of Incapacity

The burdens of life may inhibit prayer

Life is so diverse that anyone discussing it must content himself with striking a mean, knowing that general propositions never fully do justice to any individual case. Thus the reader may feel that many of the views put forward in this book are not correct or only partly so.

He will contradict, make reservations, or understand this or that differently, and he will probably be right in doing so. But if the mean has, to some extent, been correctly struck, he may find something which will be of use to him.

The problem becomes more serious when the reader declares that he can make no use at all of what has been said. It may happen, for instance, that he stands so firmly rooted in the life of prayer that the aspects advanced and advice tendered appear to him superfluous. If this is really so, there is nothing further to add, and he should not hesitate to lay this book aside. He may have an unusual disposition or special religious faculties or spiritual problems which are out of the common run. Or he may live in special circumstances which can be judged only in their own context. To begin with, one would have to say to such a person that, after all, the normal standards apply to him and that therefore he should not so easily look upon his case as exceptional. But if it should really prove to be so, then he must seek more personal advice as to how to deal with his situation.

Finally, there is always the possibility of a reader declaring that he is simply unable to pray and that what is said here either makes no sense or is impossible for him. This inability to pray is something which may happen in one form or another to any one of us and probably not only once but often. We will therefore explore it more thoroughly.

Life does not flow evenly. There are times of abundance and energy, times of emptiness and lassitude, and various stages in between. We are affected by many outside influences, some helpful, some hindering, some encouraging, and some disturbing. The morning is not like the afternoon, nor is the day like the night; and in the course of the year, man's mental attitude undergoes profound changes. When happily and successfully occupied, man is very different from what he is in times of inner poverty and frustration.

All this also affects prayer. It is not a robot or an electronic brain which prays, but a living human being, and everything which conditions his life must influence his prayer. There may be times when he has neither the strength nor the joy to pray and when inwardly everything seems dead. Then he may see no reason why he should persevere.

This state of mind may also be brought about by great fatigue, by uncongenial and monotonous work, through illness and physical weakness, or by unceasing worry and insoluble difficulties.

There is a saying that "sorrow draws us nearer to God," but like most sayings it is a half-truth only. The very opposite could equally well be said. Sorrow can turn us away from Him. Moral uncertainty and defeat may also strongly influence our attitude to prayer. Conscience does not work in isolation: man's moral success or failure must deeply influence the whole of his life. If he does what is right, everything else derives strength from it. If he fails, then this failure saps the whole of his life and robs his prayer of virtue and meaning. He loses the inclination to pray; it seems to him pointless because he has shut himself away from the holy sphere in which prayer operates.

Special mention must be made of those emotional maladjustments which come under the heading of melancholia or depression. They are important in this context because it is people of vivid religious sensibility who are prone to them, and also because they involve that very side of the psyche in which the religious impulse originates.

The melancholic has an extremely vulnerable psyche. He experiences life more vividly than other people (the beautiful, the luminous, and the great, as well as the depressing, the ugly, and the cruel) and he does this in a way which overstresses and overaccentuates everything and strains his inner resources too severely.

Everything touches him more closely, excites him more profoundly, wounds him more deeply, and leaves on him a more lasting impression than on people of a more balanced disposition. The melancholic frequently has a very vivid imagination, coupled with a powerful desire for the unattainable. All this often results in a great deal of disappointment and sorrow.

A creative talent, whether in the realm of people or of things, often goes together with melancholic tendencies, which then have to be accepted as the price of the creative gift. The hours of abundance and accomplishment must be paid for with those of emptiness and inner distress. Frequently, too, the melancholic is a person with a great capacity for love. This love is extremely demanding and vulnerable and contains within it greater possibilities of sorrow than of joy. Or he may long to be able to love, knowing what it would be like if he could, but knowing, too, that he cannot do it.

A good deal more could be said about this, but whatever the kind of melancholia and whatever its roots, it is invariably characterized by periods in which everything becomes dark, in which color and beauty vanish, in which life loses its meaning and man feels himself imprisoned in a void. When this happens he is lost to prayer, for not only have words become meaningless but the consciousness of the reality of God has vanished. Man stands in a desert, a burden to himself. Religion not only palls but provokes opposition and rebellion, and the only things which seem to retain some meaning are work or a round of pleasure.

Perseverance overcomes most obstacles to prayer

If we ask ourselves what ought to be done at such times, the answer must once again be restricted to general terms.

Above all one ought not to give in too quickly. The difficulties often appear greater than they really are and to pull oneself together may be enough in order to break the spell. It is worth recalling here that which has been said several times in this book: man, on the whole, does not enjoy prayer.

Perseverance, therefore, and faithful adherence to discipline are very important, for although prayer may become wearisome and seem devoid of meaning, this discipline of prayer has a powerful effect. It increases self-confidence and strength and helps to form real stability in religious matters. When St. Anthony the Hermit emerged from a period of great distress and temptation, he asked, "Where wast Thou, O Lord, in those days?" and received the answer, "Closer than ever before."[89] There are times in which we must live by faith alone; in them the seed of the future puts out its roots.

In times of moral defeat, when the consciousness of sin and of the consequent separation from God makes prayer seem impossible, we must try not to be too sensitive with ourselves. If we were able to do wrong in the sight of God, we must be able to bear this wrong before Him. A consciousness of guilt and hurt pride should not be allowed to become a barrier between us and God. Not only can such a barrier become permanent, but the inner disinclination to pray may use it as a convenient excuse to avoid the toil of prayer. Anyone who has reason for self-reproach should admit his guilt and start afresh without allowing it to interfere with his normal life of prayer. If in doing so he experiences remorse or shame, this is as it should be and he must bear it.

Sometimes it is useful to change the wording of our prayers — the new and unfamiliar stimulates our interest — or their form might be changed. Instead of praying in the usual sense, we should read devotional works, trying to find through them the way to God. One can withdraw to some quite simple but powerful prayers. How divinely true and great the Lord's Prayer is one realizes by the fact that it is wholeheartedly acceptable when all other prayers have palled. The same holds good for the prayer "Glory be to the Father and to the Son and to the Holy Spirit" or for some of the very simple Psalms (such as the so-called Graduals[90]).

When all is to no avail, one should at least kneel or stand before God and say, "I know that I ought to pray, but I am unable to do so." This at least establishes our obligation to pray.

[89]*The Life of St. Anthony* (attributed to St. Athanasius), Ch. 10.
[90]Pss. 119-133 (RSV: Pss. 120-134).

Perseverance can strengthen weakened faith

What happens if we do not have enough faith? Prayer speaks to the God who declares Himself in the Scriptures; but only by faith are we convinced of this truth. What happens if our faith falters, if it is not even properly established or still only partly formed? In such a case, how can we pray? Here it is not merely a question of whether our faith has sufficient strength to carry our prayer but whether we can reconcile it with our conscience to pray at all. Faith is connected with truth; but if we try to pray, being unsure of the truth, our conscience may accuse us of a lack of honesty. What then? Here the question becomes much more difficult. Previously we discussed the conflict between what we ought to do and what we can and will do; faith was not lacking, but the heart lacked the will or the capability. Here there is a conflict between what we feel we ought to do and what is the right thing to do. This is a more complex moral conflict.

Above all, we must try to understand that faith is itself life and as such undergoes change and evolution. Faith is not like empirical knowledge, established once and for all, whatever course life may take (like, for instance, the multiplication tables which, once learned, are known for good, irrespective of how we feel). Faith is *effected* by the forces of the mind and heart, by judgment and loyalty — that is to say, by the wholeness of our inner life — so that everything which happens in this inner life *affects* faith. Therefore, uncertainties, perplexities, and resistances are bound to arise. Our inner faculties may be exhausted or we may be entering a new phase of life; we may find ourselves in different surroundings and thus be influenced by new contacts. All this may be unsettling but is fundamentally quite natural and must be treated as such. Faith and prayer must persevere together, for faith is not a feeling or experience in its own right but a bridge between the believer and God. This bridge must remain even if the feeling changes or disappears. Indeed, it is the very nature of faith to persevere, for faith is not rooted in emotion but in character, not in experience but in loyalty; in short, not in the changeable but in the constant elements of life. For faith is "the victory which overcometh the world."[91] *World* in this context is not only people and things, events and circumstances outside, but above all *we ourselves*, our own life with all its tensions, weaknesses, and fluctuations.

So we must not pander to our own weaknesses but, taking a firm hold of ourselves, must stand our ground and endure.

Difficulties should not cause loss of faith

It becomes far more difficult to hold firm when faith appears to be shaken in its very roots and, for example, the truths revealed in the Scriptures seem to have lost their meaning. Deep conflicts may then arise between the demands of faith and of man's own integrity, between his sense of religious duty and his general state of mind. Of course, he ought not to force himself in what at the moment seems impossible; on the other hand, for the sake of particular difficulties he must not give up faith altogether. If certain articles of faith (such as, for instance, the divinity of Christ or the mystery of the holy Mass) have become strange to him, he must concentrate on other truths which still have meaning for him (such as, for example, Divine Providence or reward and punishment in the afterlife).

He must try to clarify his beliefs and from there go on to think, to study, to talk with authoritative people — in short, he should take as much trouble over matters of faith as he would over the

[91] 1 John 5:4.

treatment of a serious illness or the solution of a grave professional problem affecting his whole life. The same applies to prayer. It may happen that the figure of Christ becomes incomprehensible to him and that he therefore finds it difficult to pray to the Son; in this case he should concentrate more on the Father. Or the figure of the Father may become strange but the thought of the Holy Spirit still means something to him; then he must turn to Him and ask for light. He must establish which of his beliefs he really can build on and start praying from there. The truths of faith are all inter-locked. Fundamentally there is only one truth — one God in Three Persons, who reveals Himself in Christ and leads the world to salvation. If one aspect of this truth comes to life in prayer, it sheds its light on the others and gradually they all revive.

We must bear in mind that faith itself depends on prayer. It is not as if there was a ready-made faith which prays or does not pray as it pleases. Prayer — prayer in any form — is the basic act of faith as breathing is the basic act of life. Hence the struggle for faith — the searching, thinking, sorting out — must somehow be translated into prayer or establish contact with it. The analogy of breath is very apt, for as we have pointed out earlier on, while there is life there is breath and through breath life renews itself. When life becomes weak it does not cease to breathe; it continues to the utmost of its capacity, restoring its strength thereby. It is similar with faith: when it weakens, we should pray to the best of our ability, restoring our faith thereby.

The same applies to those who do not yet have any faith but are searching for it. It is important that they should not merely think and read about faith and discuss it; they should also dwell in prayer on it. But this should be done honestly; they cannot expect to anticipate, in prayer, certainties which they do not yet possess by faith. They must therefore establish a starting-point in their minds from which they can pray: to the living God or the mystery of grace or — if it is still no more than that — to what, however remote and glimmering, they conceive to be the essential reality. If all they could say to this unknown Deity were such words as "Thou Unknown God, if Thou art, Thou shouldst know that I am ready for Thee. Make me understand," this would be real prayer.

It is important that prayer and conduct should be closely linked and especially so in times of doubt and difficulty. When a man for the sake of his soul carries out a duty more conscientiously, overcomes temptation with greater determination, or is more charitable and magnanimous toward others than he would normally be, this also affects his prayer. It opens new vistas to him, purifies his judgment, and increases his spiritual power.

Reverence is possible even when prayer is not

Admittedly, there are times when prayer can do very little and there are circumstances in which man is altogether unable to pray — because he either does not know where to turn or his sense of propriety forbids him to approach God. Nevertheless, there remain for him at such times certain hidden substitutes for prayer.

He can, for example, acknowledge the sublime with special reverence wherever he encounters it and in so doing render homage to the mystery which is behind all that is noble on earth. He may make a special effort to honor all men, carefully avoiding offense in his relations with them and acknowledging the dignity that even the lowliest has. He may pay attention to the delicate, the defenseless, and the tender, or be especially heedful of physical and, even more, of mental suffering. The main thing about this attitude is its intent. It aims through earthly things at things holy and divine to which, for the time being, it has no direct access. This piety can take the form of reverence toward all living things, an endeavor not to harm or destroy anything. There is nothing sentimental about this; on the contrary, it is something very calm and genuine, something born of strength — although a strength which, to be sure, has not yet found its proper channel.

Art in one of its many forms — a painting, for instance, or a piece of music or poetry — may be a means of help at such times. Not that art can be considered as a form of religion or religion be replaced by art. Nevertheless, in times of inner difficulty some people are helped by the atmosphere and radiation of truth contained in a fine work of art. This intimation of the holy, unless the experience is confined to the merely aesthetic, can have the effect of a hidden prayer.

9

The Overall Pattern
of Christian Prayer Life

Personal prayer

This book deals with personal prayer which, however, is only one thread in the whole pattern of Christian devotion. Here in our final chapter, therefore, we will try to outline this greater design.

In personal prayer the individual faces God. God has created him and called him into a special relationship in grace with Him. It is by virtue of this relationship, in which God meets each one of us directly, that we rise to the dignity of being individuals at all — of being individual selves. It finds its expression in personal prayer, which is a dialogue between the *one* individual and God.

The worshipper, of course, includes in this dialogue his relatives, friends, people in distress, and so forth; the more selfless he is, the wider the range of his concern and his prayer for others. But in the final analysis, he is alone with God.

We can rightly apply here that expression which originated with the first hermits in the Egyptian desert, was recoined later by

St. Augustine, and in modern times was newly formulated by Cardinal Newman: "God and my soul and nothing else besides."

Personal prayer is effected in the holy and intimate solitude which encloses God and man — Him and the particular individual — each time anew. Men do not stand before God in droves, but each one is present before Him as though he were the only one. The perfect formulation of this relationship is contained in the wonderful sentence in the book of Revelation: "He that hath an ear, let him hear what the Spirit saith to the churches: to him that overcometh, I will give the hidden manna, and will give him a white counter, and in the counter, a new name written, which no man knoweth, but he that receiveth it."[92]

Personal prayer obeys certain laws, and in these pages we have tried to describe the conditions under which it operates and in which it bears fruit. These conditions are formulated in the teaching of the Scriptures, in practical rules which Christian experience has evolved through many centuries, and by certain standards of reason and wisdom which govern all spiritual activity.

Nevertheless, personal prayer is free in a very special sense and the only purpose of discipline is to safeguard that freedom. The more sincere it is, the less we can prescribe how it should be done; it assumes the form appropriate to the individual's inner condition, to his experience, and the circumstances in which he stands. Hence the prayer which may be appropriate at one time may not be so at another; and the prayer which is appropriate for one person may not meet the needs of someone else.

When prayer does not find its proper freedom of expression it becomes uncertain, monotonous, and dull. Training should help our personal prayer to become original and sure of itself. At the

[92]Rev. 2:17.

same time, personal prayer is a duty — as has been repeatedly stressed — and if this conception is lost it tends to become undisciplined and sterile. The form which this duty takes depends on the individual make-up and circumstances of the pious person, and its particular virtue lies in the fact that this person, in his irreplaceable uniqueness, should perform it.

Liturgical prayer

Besides personal prayer there is the prayer of the Liturgy. If we want to be quite precise we ought not to say the *prayer of the Liturgy* but the *liturgical actions*, for therein lies the essence of the Liturgy. This is especially true of the Sacrifice of the Mass, which fulfills our Lord's instructions, given to His Apostles at the Last Supper: "*Do* this in remembrance of me." From this central action, the prayers of the Mass arise.

The same holds good for the sacraments. They, too, are essentially ritual actions instituted by God but performed by man for the benefit of man.

From this center the Liturgy goes out like ripples into the world, expressed in various symbolic and holy customs which permeate the Christian life. Their foundation is always ritual action on which rests prayer.

There are, of course, certain parts of the Liturgy which consist mainly of prayer in its own right — for instance, the choral offices performed in cathedrals and abbeys or said as the Breviary by the priest to himself. But these choral offices are frequently interspersed with action; they are performed in given parts of the church; certain climaxes are underlined by symbolic rites (such as censing of the altar) and are accompanied by gestures (such as the sign of the Cross, bowing, genuflecting, rising, sitting, standing up, and so forth).

The difference between personal and liturgical prayer

Personal prayer is said in silence by the heart or spoken by the mouth and is accompanied only by the merest hint of gesture or action. The Liturgy, on the other hand, is above all a system of actions, of which prayer constitutes only one element.

Personal prayer and the Liturgy are the two main spheres of religious life, each one having its own roots and character and each its unique significance. In personal prayer man is alone with God and himself. The Liturgy, however, is a united prayer of the Christian community. In the Liturgy it is not *I* but *we*; and the *we* does not merely signify that many individuals are congregated. It is not a sum of individuals but a wholeness: the Church.

It exists even when one or the other, or many, have divorced themselves from its body, for it does not have its origin in the desire of the individual for community but in the creative will of God, which embraces the whole of mankind. It was founded by Christ, came into being on the day of Pentecost, and will exist whether the generations want it or not.

Called by Christ to be the bearer of His message, it holds authority over the individual and the many. As Christ said: "And if he will not hear them: tell the church. And if he will not hear the church, let him be to thee as the heathen and publican."[93] The Church comprises not only the totality of mankind in Christ but, as St. Paul and St. John teach, the totality of the world. Thus in the final analysis the Church is the sanctified whole, the new creation in the governance of the Holy Spirit.[94]

On the other hand, the Church does not exist outside the individual but within him. We are — each one of us — members

[93]Matt. 18:17.
[94]Col. 1:3-20; Eph. 1:3-23.

of the Church inasmuch as we belong to it, and individuals inasmuch as we face God alone. It is this Church — this universal Church — which acts and speaks in the Liturgy. It follows that the attitude of the individual when he participates in a liturgical rite and joins in liturgical prayer is different from his attitude in personal prayer.

It is not something beside or in contradiction to the latter but rather is its necessary counterweight in the pattern of Christian existence. Through the Liturgy man steps out of his separateness and becomes a part of the whole: a living organ through which the total message of the Church is expressed and enacted.

Liturgical prayer and ritual are obligatory

In this light, everything which comes under the heading of *discipline* assumes a new significance. The prayer of the individual requires some discipline in order that it may remain wholesome and orderly; apart from that it should spring from the originality of the inner urge.

On the other hand, in the sphere of liturgical prayer and ritual, this kind of originality would not make sense and would lead to arbitrariness and confusion. From long experience, therefore, and by repeated examination and revision, the Church has shaped and reshaped the liturgical order. This order is more than a guide; it is a ruling which it is our duty to obey.

In the Liturgy there is no room for variations or, more precisely, no room for individual variations; for, of course, it does contain a certain kind of freedom. This freedom does not arise from the will of the individual but from that of the Church, in which the Holy Spirit reigns.

It expresses itself by the absence of aim. The Liturgy does not wish to achieve anything; it merely wants to dwell in the presence of God, to breathe and unfold there, to love and to praise Him. This freedom operates in broad sweeps and on a worldwide scale through the centuries.

Thus its action and scope go far beyond the considerations of the individual and therefore assume the character of law in relation to him. Hence, in a much stricter sense than in personal prayer, liturgical prayer and ritual are a *duty*. By ancient tradition, the holy functions are regulated in every detail. The texts have been tried and proven by the Church and must be spoken exactly as they are recorded in the liturgical books.

The believer who takes part in liturgical worship will do so all the more correctly and single-mindedly the more sincerely he is able to detach himself from his own personal desires. In personal prayer he may obey the promptings of his heart. In liturgical worship, however, he must open himself to a different kind of impulse which comes from a more powerful source: namely, the heart of the Church which beats through the ages. Here it does not matter what his personal tastes are, what wants he may have, or what particular cares occupy his mind. All this he must leave behind and enter into the powerful rhythm of liturgical rites. It is precisely by this abandonment that he experiences the most important effect of the Liturgy — the detachment and liberation from the narrow self.

We have mentioned that the main accent in the Liturgy is on the holy acts. We want to return to this proposition because we have largely lost sight of the concept behind it. The main accent of religious life has shifted more and more onto the individual inwardness, the realm of experience, of thinking and wanting. Hand in hand with this change of emphasis has gone a trend to regard the Liturgy mainly as a means of instruction and edification. Its true significance is that it is the symbolic re-enacting of Christian religious events in a substantial, spiritual-material form.

God has declared Himself to man not only by inward revelation but also by historical words and actions and, conclusively, in the person, life, and destiny of Christ. In Him the Epiphany — the showing forth of the invisible God — has been achieved. Thus also the realization of the message of Christ to us happens in historical — that is, spiritual-material — form.

The Church is not only a spiritual body, a communion in faith and love, but stands visibly, authoritatively, and responsibly in the history of the world. Christ's heritage is entrusted to the Church. In Her lives the transfigured Lord, constantly bringing His redeeming destiny into our earthly existence. We make this destiny our own in different ways: by individual thought and appreciation, by following His example, and also by specific actions which are performed here and now in a precise order laid down by the Church. For example, Christ has risen once and for all and our faith can be assured of this at any time.

Nevertheless, it is a fact that the truth, the grace, and the sanctifying power of the Resurrection are brought home to the faithful in a special way at a particular moment — in the liturgical celebration of Easter. He said, "For where there are two or three gathered together in my name, there am I in the midst of them."[95] In the Easter Liturgy, He comes to the celebrating faithful in the full glory of His Resurrection. When the *Exsultet* is sung and the Paschal candle is newly lit, its radiance gradually filling the entire space of the church, the congregation knows that "now it is Easter and the glory of the Resurrection is among us."

This is more than an instructional or edifying allegory; it is truth — the truth of liturgical rite. This truth is largely lost to modern man. He has no more an understanding for symbolism. He

[95]Matt. 18:20.

has forgotten how to look for the inner meaning of outward events, how to partake of the divine contents in concrete action, and how — on a different plan — to continue what St. John expressed in his letter: "That which was from the beginning, which we have heard, which we have seen with our eyes, which we have looked upon, and our hands have handled, of the word of life."[96] He wants only to talk, to hear, to think, and to judge.

This is not enough, and he ought to revive those powers so long neglected and those faculties which he has allowed to atrophy. He must learn afresh not merely to think about symbolic forms but to see and enter into them; not, during holy ceremonies, to ask what this or that detail means, but to join in with them and thus fully to partake of their meaning and contents. It is expected of the celebrant of the Liturgy that he should fully understand its meaning and conduct its services in a manner which enables those who are of goodwill to hear the Word of Life, to see it with their eyes and to handle it with their hands.[97]

Forms of popular devotion

Liturgical and personal prayer do not completely exhaust the possibilities of religious life. There is a third form which, for want of a better term, we shall call *popular devotion*. To it belongs Matins and Vespers, family prayers, the recitation of the Rosary, and the majority of religious folk customs.

This kind of devotion cannot easily be defined. It is best described by saying that it lies between liturgical and personal prayer, but is distinct from both. Compared with personal prayer it has a communal character because in it the attitude and necessity

[96]1 John 1:1.
[97]Ibid.

not of the individual but of the group comes to the fore. It is ordered by custom and rules and thereby commands a certain authority. On the other hand, it is more private than the Liturgy because the various forms of popular devotion are not the same for the whole Church nor even for a whole country, but may hold good only for a particular diocese. They may even vary from parish to parish. Thus they reflect the change of time, the local peculiarities, the diversities of daily life, and the general variety of conditions much more directly than does the Liturgy, which changes much more slowly and whose scope is much more wide.

Popular devotion is less strict than liturgical prayer. Its phrasing is looser and more expansive; imagination plays a greater part in it and the whole atmosphere is one of warmth and immediacy. On the other hand, it lacks the wide sweep of the Liturgy, its austerity and power. Popular devotion tends toward the emotional and occasionally lapses into the sentimental or the bizarre.

Popular devotion is fond of repetition. In liturgical prayer the principle that the identical thing should never be done twice holds good. In popular devotion, however, the same words recur continually. The object of popular devotion is, of course, to abide in the presence of God; however, conditions in many of the smaller parishes are such that the proper liturgical prayers — for instance, the Psalms — cannot be used to much purpose. Their place is taken by certain simple texts such as the Lord's Prayer or the Hail Mary, in which anyone can take part but which are, of course, open to the dangers of monotony and of being recited without much feeling or thought.

Restricted in its range, popular devotion has a strong local or parochial flavor. The Christian *we* is more vivid and more reassuring to the individual than in liturgical prayer. The local and intimate atmosphere which one feels in this devotion does, in fact, come not only from the more emotional character of the texts and songs, but from the much closer communal bonds which carry it. The form of these songs or hymns is popular rather than liturgical. They express with greater directness the religious impulses of the people at the expense, however, of a certain lowering of musical value and spiritual meaning.

The essential unity of prayer

The various spheres of prayer life do not stand alone but are closely interrelated. History shows how these spheres continually merge into one another. A good many features of liturgical prayer originated with the private devotion of some pious person; conversely, personal devotion has adopted liturgical features and texts. As to popular devotion, a great deal of what now forms part of the Liturgy was originally no more than the expression of the religious life of a particular diocese or country and was only adopted generally at a later date. On the other hand, many features of popular devotion are simplified versions of liturgical texts.

These could all be described as links on the historical level, but the essential connection goes far deeper. Liturgical and personal prayer mutually sustain each other. Each sphere springs from its own separate roots; yet they belong together and form the wholeness of Christian life.

In the Liturgy the Church continually enacts the holy service instituted by Christ and the individual merges into it. At the same time, in order to take part in this way and not on a purely superficial level, his own personal religious life must have independent existence. Undoubtedly it is the Church as a whole which performs this service, but it is also the Church as embodied in the individual priest or worshipper. And undoubtedly it is the worship of the Church which the Liturgy carries into effect, but it is through the inner life of each individual that it is expressed.

If the individual has not learned to face God, if his ears are not open and his lips are closed to prayer, then the liturgical service will not flow through a living channel but merely through organs of sense, thereby depriving it of all truth and significance. Only if the individual also prays as an individual can the great prayer of the Church come into its own.

Conversely, for his personal prayer the individual needs the link with the prayer of the Church — and not only in order that the faith of the Church may sustain him and that he may be included in its perpetual intercession. Here, as with all living things, strength has its own weakness. What distinguishes personal prayer — solitude, the inward encounter, freedom of movement, and originality of expression — may also become a danger. Solitude may turn into isolation, freedom into arbitrariness, originality into the bizarre. The subjective element needs to be drawn into the objective and all-embracing. The Liturgy is a canon of worship not merely in the sense that it instructs its partakers on how to perform their duty but also because it contains the imperishable standards of genuine and wholesome devotion.

There is a world of difference between *personal* and merely *subjective* prayer. Prayer deserves to be called *personal* when it arises out of the dignity of man answering for himself, from the fountainhead of his inner life, and from the immediate encounter between him and his Creator and Redeemer. Prayer must be called *subjective* when the individual merely seeks himself, putting what seems true to him and his own uncertain religious sentiments in the place of revealed truth.

Again and again the believer must step into the discipline of the Liturgy, must take part in its grandeur and in the well-defined order of its ritual. Without this, his personal prayer may be sidetracked into the sentimental, the bizarre, or even the unnatural and diseased.

The same could be said for popular devotion which, whenever the liturgical life is not properly understood and cherished, undergoes a peculiar deterioration. The pitfalls of popular devotion are poverty of intellect, unchecked fantasy, the lack of proportion, and disorder of sentiment. If popular devotion is left to the free play of direct religious impulse, the contents of its faith tend to become inadequate and its affirmations unreliable, while the repetitions accumulate and the feeling becomes spurious and sentimental. The religious life of a parish in which the Liturgy does not play its proper role and which therefore draws its nourishment mainly from popular devotion must inevitably be impoverished.

All this should not make us forget the other side of the picture. There is a form of liturgical zeal which looks upon all popular devotion as inferior or at least superfluous. It springs from the same attitude which regards personal prayer as a mere encroachment upon the Liturgy.

This is a wrong and dangerous point of view. In its own way, it resembles the attitude of the person who says: "All that is necessary is humanity as a whole. There is no need for a people. I am content with the world; I do not need a homeland." Popular devotion is to religious life what the link with people, family, country, and home is to the natural life. A good afternoon service worthily and piously performed, a Rosary in the evening said in the proper spirit, are beautiful, profound, and intimate — something which the Christian mind needs to remain healthy.

Romano Guardini
(1885-1968)

Although he was born in Verona, Italy, Romano Guardini grew up in Mainz, Germany, where his father was serving as Italian consul. Since his education and formation were German, he decided to remain in Germany as an adult.

After studying chemistry and economics as a youth, Guardini turned to theology and was ordained to the priesthood in 1910. From 1923 to 1939 (when he was expelled by the Nazis), Msgr. Guardini occupied a chair created for him at the University of Berlin as "professor for philosophy of religion and Catholic *Weltanschauung*." After the war, similar positions were created for him, first at the University of Tübingen and then at the University of Munich (1948-63).

Msgr. Guardini's extremely popular courses in these universities won him a reputation as one of the most remarkable and successful Catholic educators in Germany.

As a teacher, a writer, and a speaker, he was notable for being able to detect and to nurture those elements of spirituality that nourish all that is best in the life of Catholics. After the war, Msgr. Guardini's influence grew to be enormous, not only through his university positions, but also through the inspiration and guidance he gave to the post-war German Catholic Youth Movement, which enlivened the faith of countless young people.

Msgr. Guardini's writings include works on meditation, education, literature, art, philosophy, and theology. Among his dozens of books, perhaps the most famous is *The Lord*, which has been continuously in print in many languages since its first publication in 1937. Even today, countless readers continue to be transformed by these books, which combine a profound thirst for God with great depth of thought and a delightful perfection of expression. The works of Msgr. Guardini are indispensable reading for anyone who wants to remain true to the Faith and to grow holy in our age of skepticism and corrosive doubt.

SOPHIA INSTITUTE PRESS

Sophia Institute is a non-profit institution that seeks to restore man's knowledge of eternal truth, including man's knowledge of his own nature, his relation to other persons, and his relation to God.

Sophia Institute Press serves this end in a number of ways. It publishes translations of foreign works to make them accessible for the first time to English-speaking readers. It brings back into print many books that have long been out of print. And it publishes important new books that fulfill the ideals of Sophia Institute. These books afford readers a rich source of the enduring wisdom of mankind.

Sophia Institute Press makes high-quality books available to the general public by using advanced, cost-effective technology and by soliciting donations to subsidize general publishing costs. Your generosity can help us provide the public with editions of works containing the enduring wisdom of the ages. Please send your tax-deductible contribution to the address noted below. Your questions, comments, and suggestions are also welcome.

For your free catalog, call:
Toll-free: 1-800-888-9344

or write:

SOPHIA INSTITUTE PRESS
BOX 5284
MANCHESTER, NH 03108

Sophia Institute is a tax-exempt institution as defined by the Internal Revenue Code, Section 501(c)(3). Tax I.D. 22-2548708.